Dear Michael,

You are so creative we thought you might enjoy this book —

Enjoy —

Love always

Grandma J. Grandpa ♡ —

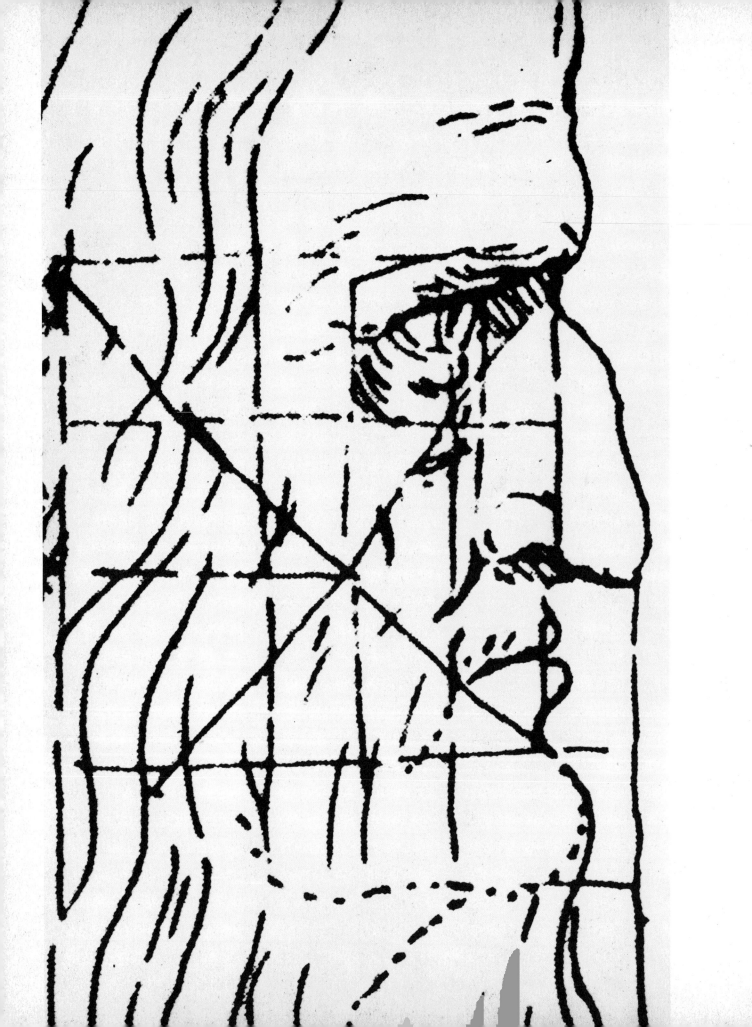

LEONARDO'S INVENTIONS

Text by

Jean Mathé

Translated by David Mac Rae

Crescent Books
New York

First published by Productions Liber S.A., Fribourg, 1980
Copyright © MCMLXXX by Productions Liber S.A. and Editions Minerva S.A.
Library of Congress Catalog Card Number: 79-57033
ISBN: 0-517-30712 X
This edition is published by Crescent Books,
a division of Crown Publishers, Inc.
a b c d e f g h
Printed and bound in Italy by L.E.G.O. - Vicenza

The sixty-seven years of the turbulent and impassioned life of Leonardo da Vinci took place against the background of the seething activity of the Renaissance, one of the most brilliantly creative periods in the history of mankind.

It is hardly surprising that his exuberant genius flourished joyfully in such a setting, which provided him with the breath of inspiration for the often irrational and enthusiastic projects of this amazing visionary.

However, the few small houses, built of rust-colored stone, of the hamlet of Anchiano, near Vinci, some twenty miles from Florence, seemed quite remote from all this intellectual ferment when Leonardo was born there on April 15, 1452. The aura of mystery which surrounded his entire life, and work started at his very birth. He was the illegitimate son of a mother of whom nothing at all was known – not even her name, age or personality. Tradition merely made her a maid at an inn, named Caterina.

His father, on the other hand, was, if not famous, at least well-placed in society, being a rich, respected lawyer; Ser Piero was 25 years old when Leonardo was born. He was an exceptionally vigorous man who had four legal wives and twelve children, the last of whom was born when he was seventy-five, two years before his death.

In such a turbulent age the status of bastard was not a stigma. So Ser Piero calmly recognized Leonardo, but entrusted him to a peasant couple in Vinci, where he spent the early years of his childhood. It was only when his first wife was found to be sterile that he moved to recover his son and instal him in the family house, a short while later simply leaving him there while he went off to Florence to arrange some highly lucrative business deals.

One can only imagine Leonardo's awakening to the world about him among the rolling green hills of Tuscany which held a special appeal for him, as he ran around on the foothills of Monte Albano, amongst the low vegetation dotted with olive trees and cypresses.

This region, which is still unspoilt, having been spared the worst ravages of modern tourism, is one of the finest in Italy, its charm unaffected by the passage of time.

The modern visitor can readily understand how Leonardo could have been influenced by such a place. It was here that he acquired his passion for nature, and that his senses awakened to the marvelous world of plants, birds and rocks – all of which were both esthetically and intellectually pleasing to him, as he sought to unravel the enigma of their underlying essence.

Leonardo's mind was to be deeply and permanently impressed by this magical beauty and these profound questions.

This was particularly true because he did not receive a conventional education during his early years, when his formative influences were solely empirical, instinctive and sensorial.

He never learnt Latin – a fact which he always regretted as it denied him access, in the distinctly humanistic world in which he lived, to the traditional sources of classical culture and the heritage of antiquity.

It seems quite likely, however, that his originality of mind, his independence of thought and his tendency to question anything which he had not himself verified or experienced, derived from that lonely childhood in the depths of the countryside, where the scents of the flowers, the rustling of the wind and the colors of the sky were his only teachers.

At the age of fifteen his father, having noticed his artistic gifts, took him to Florence and had him admitted to one of the painting studios which were prospering in the city which was then at the peak of its magnificence.

It had become a traditional practice for the sons of distinguished families to take part in the artistic ferment which made the City of the Medicis the crucible of the Renaissance : there were few truly outstanding artists, but large numbers of wonderful craftsmen.

Leonardo grew up to be a handsome adolescent, intelligent and gifted, with immense charm and an impressive presence. Beneath his worldly exterior and pleasing social gifts – he sang and played the lute – lay hidden, even then, a tormented and lonely soul.

He was admitted to the studio of Andrea del Verrochio, one of the most famous in Florence. Students entered at the age of fourteen and, after six years of work under the guidance of the master, they were eligible for membership of St Luke's Guild, which enabled them to use the official title of Painter and open their own studios. The studio of Verrochio was remarkable for its quality and its universality: besides painting, the students also learnt sculpture, the craft of the goldsmith, techniques for working with bronze and smelting. It was even possible to become involved in the creation of costumes and the organization of the lavish galas so popular in the courts of the Renaissance.

Leonardo fitted perfectly into all this creative ferment, and soon worked on the commissions which had been entrusted to the studio. According to tradition Verrochio, upset by his pupil's extraordinary gifts, gradually abandoned painting himself, finding that the disciple transcended the master.

In actual fact, however, Leonardo always stayed on good terms with Verrochio, whom he continued to visit after leaving and setting up his own studio. He was twenty years old. It was about this time that

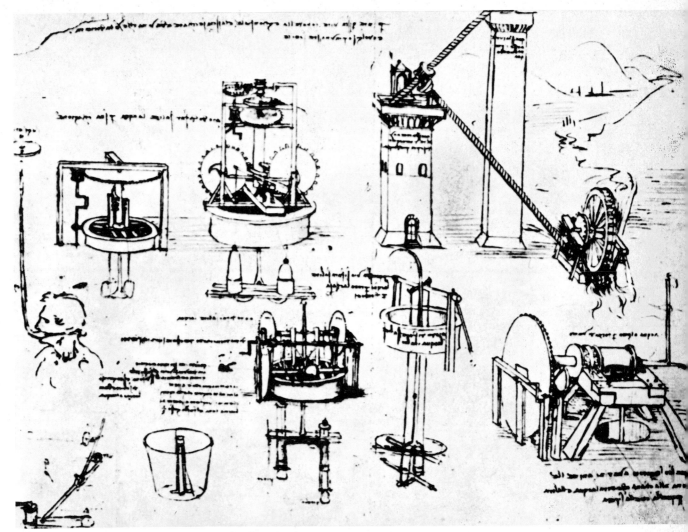

Various types of wheeled pumps.

he became friendly with Botticelli and visited all the artistic centers of Florence.

Such contacts were necessary because in those days theory and artistic precepts were handed down by word of mouth; there were virtually no manuals of style, with the possible exception of the *Craftsmen's Treatise,* written in 1437 by Cennino Chennini, which was the apprentice's Bible.

It was therefore through direct contact with Donatello, Brunelleschi, Alberti, Benedetto dell' Abacco, and so many others, that Leonardo brought his art to maturity, by the meeting of his own genius with the influence of his great contemporaries.

Yet his own studio, which he opened in 1476, was not the success he had hoped for. He kept out of politics, and was thus ignored by the Medicis – so much so that he was not even listed among the best Tuscan artists who were invited to decorate the Vatican.

Together with a charge of homosexuality which excluded him from official favor, the indifference of the Medicis drove him to seek protection from other sources.

He found it in 1482 in Milan, with the powerful Duke Ludovico Sforza, and left his beloved Florence for the capital of Lombardy.

He stayed there for twenty years, during which time he achieved the fame and success which had eluded him hitherto. He was thirty. This was to be his most fertile and enthusiastic creative period.

Having been given the curious title of Engineer and Military Expert by Sforza, he worked on everything, following his universal bent in a thousand directions: as painter, architect, inspired mechanical engineer, he was to be the Grand Master of Feasts at the court.

He soon noticed however, that his protector, though apparently attentive to his ideas, virtually ignored his visionary projects, preferring instead to set him to work on a bathroom for a mistress!

However, Sforza did commission him to build a huge equestrian statue with which to glorify his reign. Leonardo spent about sixteen years working on this megalomanic project of the *cavallo,* inventing hoisting devices and smelting processes, but never getting beyond the stage of making sketches which, though fascinating, remained sterile.

He was constantly interrupted in his work, being summoned to Pavia as technical adviser for the construction of the cathedral, then back to Milan for the wedding celebrations of Ludovico Sforza, yet he accumulated a fantastic harvest of sketches on all the subjects which occured to him: mathematics, optics, mechanics, anatomy. He sought the supposedly identical underlying mechanisms of nature and man.

Despite its magnificence, however, the court of Milan used his abilities without ever taking him seriously.

In 1490 he already found himself in the position of Master of Ceremonies without any official commissions, while increasingly poorly paid by the duke, who proved to be a tight-fisted patron.

About this time he became involved with a handsome, unstable youth named Salai, whom he supported and protected for twenty-five years!

In 1499, when Sforza was defeated by the French and overthrown, a disillusioned Leonardo, now almost poor – he had not been paid for two years! – left Milan and took refuge in Florence. From his seventeen years in the duke's employ he took with him many broken illusions and an enormous mass of sketches which bore witness to his aborted projects.

Passing through Venice and Mantua he reached the Tuscan capital in 1500, accompanied by the inseparable Salai, who was both valet and parasite.

He was received with polite deference, but nothing more.

How his city had changed! Once Lorenzo de Medicis was dead, the Medicis had been expelled. After a crisis of acute puritanism, the mystical monk Savonarola had been burnt there two years before (1498).

The brilliance and the effervescence of the *Quattrocento* were now only memories.

Verrochio and his contemporaries were dead, and the exuberant

*Plan of an experiment to measure
the muscular resistance of a bird.*

gaiety of a city alive with ideas and splendor had now given way to assiduous but humdrum toil.

In particular, the radiant twenty-five year old Michelangelo, the city's new artistic idol, had eclipsed the careworn forty-eight year old Leonardo.

However, he was received and housed in the Convent of the Annunciation, where he worked on a painting commissioned by the order.

He soon left to enlist in the service of the new strong man of Italy, Cesar Borgia, for whom he worked for eight years as Military Engineer. During a campaign at Urbino he met Macciavelli, the Florentine Chancellor, with whom he became friendly.

Much has been written about this shocking allegiance to the Borgias. There can be no doubt that Leonardo saw in Cesar Borgia, – Machiavelli's model in *The Prince* – the only leader capable of unifying Italy, which was fragmented and pulled apart into a multitude of mini-kingdoms and foreign influences.

He failed, however, in his plan, and then returned to Florence (1504), where Machiavelli had arranged for him to work with Michelangelo on the *Battle of Anghiari,* celebrating the victory of the Florentines over Milan in 1440.

But in 1506, at the request of the French who were in control of Milan, he left for that city, where he met his most faithful disciple, Melzi.

Thereafter he was under the protection of Louis XII, who named him *Painter and Engineer of the King,* a post he held until the defeat of the French at Pavia (1512).

Now that Maximilian Sforza was reigning in Milan, Leonardo once again sought a new refuge and a new host. He left for Rome, where he lived from 1513 to 1516; the new Pope, Leo X, a Medici, welcomed him warmly. He even commissioned him to do a painting. But before making even a single sketch for it, Leonardo started working on a new varnish! «This man will never finish anything» exclaimed the Pope, who thereafter lost interest in him, shifting his favor to Raphael, the new rising star.

From then on, Leonardo, who had now stopped painting altogether, amassed even greater numbers of sketches and projects, and did his famous drawings of the Deluge, an apocalyptic vision of the universe and of death which had just come close to visiting him, with a fleeting but savage attack which left one hand partially paralyzed.

It was the invitation of Francis I, his only genuine royal friend, for him to come to Amboise, that saved Leonardo from an undignified old age.

He left for France in 1516, with the indestructible Salai and the loyal Melzi. His luggage contained the impressive total of his drawings and note books which were to represent his real intellectual testament.

As Architect of the King he lived in princely style in the manor at Cloux, less than a mile from the Chateau d'Amboise, to which it was linked by a tunnel which the restless Francis I, his most sincere admirer, often took to make respectful yet excited visits to his distinguished guest. In one last flicker of his genius he planned to make the Loire and its tributaries navigable, organized the gala at Blois, and died on May 2, 1519, as a result of a stroke.

Melzi, his universal heir, inherited the master's drawings and note-books – an awesome and fabulous legacy.

One of the most unexpected paradoxes of Leonardo's work is the fact that his fame among the general public is due to his glory as a painter. In actual fact, he painted only thirty paintings in his whole life, and only a dozen or so of these are unquestionably his.

Apart from anything else, many of these canvasses were never completed. Many of them have not survived, having been lost on account of the vicissitudes of his unstable life or fallen victim to his bold and sometimes disastrous experimental technical 'inventions'.

His essential work was therefore not that of a painter, but of a humanist thinker and universal engineer who observed everything and then attempted to explain it.

On his death he left an enormous amount of notes and drawings dealing with all spheres of perception and knowledge.

Projects of his which, like so many others, remained unfinished, include: outlines of a treatise on painting, of a book on light and shadow, a smelting manual, and books on mathematics.

Above all, there was an incredible amount of scattered sketches, jotted down untidily on the pages of countless notebooks, or even on an irregular assortment of loose leaves of all dimensions and colors.

They were always accompanied by abundant notes made with a pen in that extraordinary backwards handwriting which Leonardo used in all his personal writing and which had to be read in a mirror.

Since he never knew Latin, the medium for expressing the thinking of his age, he drafted his commentaries in the vernacular Italian. It was perhaps through a need for secrecy and security that he had adopted such an original process of transcription, which made it impossible for anyone to read his notes in the normal manner; though it has been suggested that it may have been motivated by the fondness for mystery and fantasy which he always cultivated.

His sketches and drawings are always remarkably accurate and esthetically pleasing – a blend between mathematical necessity and the subconscious quest for plastic beauty which was so much a part of his being.

For Leonardo drawing was a means of expression, a script, a language more precise than any words: it was the best and most reliable way to convey ideas and sensations.

Notwithstanding the apparent disorder of his sketches, he is clearly a master of 'layout', cleverly arranging on the same sheet his notes and drawings so as to enhance the shapes and dynamism of his strokes, which virtually come alive before one's very eyes.

It was during his Milan period that he was to be most inventive, amassing an incredible harvest of ideas, for which the sketch served as both witness and depositary. Throughout his life, however, and until his dying day, he never stopped drawing and writing.

Overwhelmed by the magnitude of his responsibility and the awesome nature of his task, Melzi spent fifty years attempting to organize his fabulous inheritance, in Lombardy, in his family's castle at Vaprio.

It seems surprising that he failed to produce some kind of effective synthesis out of all these works, especially as he had lived close to Leonardo all those years, working with him on his projects and acquiring a thorough knowledge of his profound aims and motives.

There are two possible explanations for Melzi's failure: he may have been deterred and simply overcome by the disorderly mass of documents which he had to arrange in some kind of order; or the suspicion of heresy and subversion which long surrounded philosophical and scientific writings may have prevented their publication.

As for Melzi's son, he completely lost interest in the inheritance, and the priceless collections were then lost, stolen or sold: at any rate, they were dispersed.

A certain Pompeo Leoni managed, however, to recover ten volumes and arranged for them to be sold in Spain. It was he who – by cutting and pasting – pieced together the Windsor Collection, containing the anatomical drawings and the *Codex Atlanticus,* dealing with machines. The contents were, however, very loosely arranged, without any chronological order.

In fact it was not until the end of the nineteenth century that those of Leonardo's notes and drawings which had survived these vicissitudes were assembled for study once more. They account for less than one third of his total output.

The modern reader, on considering these works, is left with two opposing impressions: a feeling of failure, of incompleteness, and hopelessness, in the light of so many inspired but disorderly efforts leading to a mass of projects which for the most part remained on paper. But also fervent admiration for these superb manifestations of an exceptional faculty for universal comprehension.

The diffuse nature of Leonardo's efforts reminds one of Aristotle, yet his unitary conception of the world shows that he is a disciple of Plato.

He attempted the synthesis of the ancient theory of the elements (water – earth – fire) and the Platonic superposition of the macrocosm of the universe and the microcosm of man.

For him Nature was a living giant: just like man, it has breathing (the winds), circulation (the tides of the oceans) and motion (earthquakes and natural disasters).

This was the origin of his two great passions: the need to know the anatomy of man and the forces governing the laws of the universe.

For Leonardo the essence of any true knowledge was mathematics. It was the basis of all understanding, of any explanation of the visible phenomena and the underlying mechanisms of beings and things.

It was also the origin of all construction and human creation. This arid conception was of course tempered by the need for visual representation of knowledge.

The science of Leonardo da Vinci is a 'visualized' science. Painting, drawing were for him graphic tools which made such a materialization possible, together with the pragmatic and concrete representation of abstract theory.

Leonardo looked at the universe: he observed, saw and thought. He then conveyed his thoughts, using the strokes of his pen to bring to life ideas and mechanisms.

All of this leads to a strange blending of layers of reality and abstraction, thought and vision, art and science, of which he was seeking a synthesis.

Despite the high importance which he attached to mathematics he was never able to liberate himself from his quest for beauty; the result of his endeavors is that the most recalcitrant of the laws of physics becomes, before our very eyes, a genuine work of art, thanks to the magic of an inspired drawing.

One has merely to consider his sketches for *The Flood* or *The Tempests* to perceive the theatrical, dramatic – one might almost say 'Romantic' – inspiration which permeates his whole conception of the universe.

What could be called Leonardo's 'scientific research' was channeled into two very different directions:

On the one hand, the study of physical phenomena and secret forces (gravity, traction, etc.) which determine the static and dynamic states of bodies: the secret world of invisible and abstract forces.

On the other hand, the observation of visible nature (botany, geology, anatomy, etc.) which makes up our real, concrete world.

The same research, however, occurs in this apparent divergence, as the forces of the abstract physical laws also determine our universality.

Not being imbued with Latin and with classical culture like all the scholarly philosophers of his age, he had not been lumbered with the usual traditional assortment of cultural deadwood, and kept intact the independence of mind which was necessary for intellectual skepticism.

He thus tried to establish a new scientific culture, cleansed of conventional notions, in which everything would be observed, verified and tested before being accepted.

That led to the creation of a technology which was the practical application of abstract theories and the privileged domain of Leonardo.

For him mechanics was the fruit of mathematics; it was also proof of one's mastery of the fundamental laws of the universe and one's control over its forces – in his eyes the noblest accomplishment of man.

In this way, throughout his drawings in which he reveals his role as a precursor or a visionary, one witnesses a veritable procession of all the elements of the craft of the 'engineer' – in his eyes, the most meritorious of all because the hand creates and extends that which has been discovered by the mind.

His love of the concrete and the pragmatic, which led him to 'construct', was a way of verifying the abstract.

There was no sphere of industry or mechanics in which he did not demonstrate his prophetic genius. Does it matter, then, if he produced only incomplete or unfulfilled projects? Since his death Italian engineers have been able to build, perfectly, working models on the basis of his drawings; thus providing, five centuries later, spectacular posthumous confirmation of his merits.

One can safely say that this dazzling array of drawings which illustrate his view of applied mechanics, is truly the essential part of Leonardo's work.

Perhaps better than any other section of his work it expresses his

universal quest: a means of giving man, through a knowledge and mastery of the laws of his universe, the tools he needs in order to become, in his turn, a creator.

It was in Milan that Leonardo first saw the potential of great hydraulic projects.

In his native Tuscany the Arno had always tumbled playfully through the hills, whereas the Po had, for more than two centuries, been regulated by dams which controlled its flow and irrigated its plain.

With his usual attraction for new problems which excited his curiosity, Leonardo soon proposed original and realistic solutions, some of which were on an astonishingly large scale.

It is true that, in the sphere of hydraulic architecture, he had before his eyes the ancient structures built empirically by his Roman ancestors: bridges, dams and aqueducts, in excellent condition, were strewn about the Italian landscape.

Yet his personal contribution was, as usual, the search for a better understanding of the laws which governed the static and dynamic states of fluids.

This was an extraordinary development, as before his time the scientists of ancient Rome and Greece, doubtless irked by the fluid properties of water, had been unable to formulate the laws or even the principles of its flow.

Apart from the obvious and empirically verifiable notion of communicating vessels, classical mathematical science, being based on fixed geometries and measurable entities, had run into the intractable problem of the study of the behavior of water, the elusive element.

Leonardo worked in two very different but complementary directions: on the one hand, hydraulic and hydrodynamic research leading to certain elementary but indispensable general laws; and on the other hand, large hydraulic projects applying these principles in practice.

To understand, of course, it is essential to start by observing, then experimenting in order to verify the theoretical hypoteses to which he had been led by his intuition and his visual observation.

Using the design of the earliest hydraulic machines made by Heron of Alexandria in the 1st century AD, he soon anticipated two fundamental laws of fluid statics: 1) a liquid does not exert the same

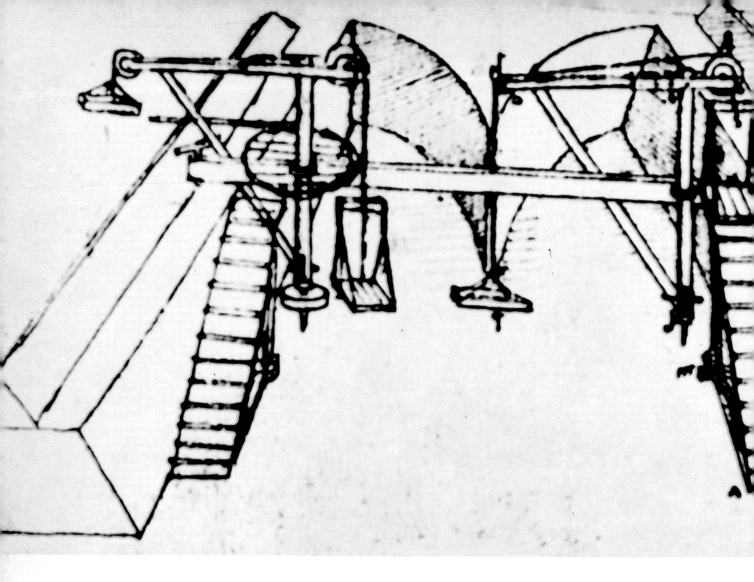

pressure on all points of the receptacle which contains it; 2) the greater the depth of the water, the higher the pressure. Moreover, the depth being equal, water gushes most strongly from the narrowest opening.

Releasing water through different openings, of varying diameter and height, he studied the trajectory of the jet and assumed that it must be affected by atmospheric pressure – a conclusion later to be arrived at by Torricelli.

The first practical application of these studies was an improved method for assessing the flow in irrigation channels – a crucial matter, since the duchy of Milan was in the habit of selling irrigation water by making lateral openings in these channels.

He studied waterfalls and discovered their immense power: the water fell, he concluded, because it was heavy and this impulse took the form of force of impact, used in the paddle-wheels – ancestors of modern turbines – which powered all sorts of mills.

He worked to measure the forces applied to the bottoms of receptacles, on dikes and on dams. This led to the birth of a series of measuring devices which made it possible to make a more or less approximate measurement of the speed, power and flow of fluids.

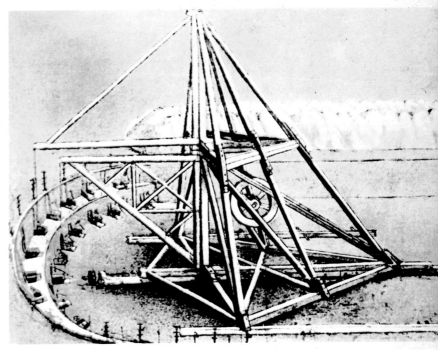

Left: plan of a machine designed to transport supplies for the building of a canal.
Above: this machine, based on a similar idea, is thought to have been connected with the digging of a canal between Florence and the sea – a project which was entrusted to Leonardo.

He was the first to conceive the precise difference of flows as a function of the diameter of the tubing through the which the fluid passed.

He was also the first to invent a 'meter', calculating the flow and the quantity of water distributed for irrigation, and made more equitable billing for such water a possibility.

He designed tubes with spiral interiors which began turning when filled from the top; he also used them to measure the power of waterfalls; the faster they turned the greater was the power of the fall.

He was clearly fascinated by rivers, waves and, in particular, by the motion of the tides which he rightly saw as an immense reservoir of energy. The beating of the sea reminded him of those of the human heart and of circulation.

His reputation as a hydraulic expert was such that he was constantly receiving invitations to study projects involving irrigation or the regularization of rivers.

His most ambitious project was to make the Arno navigable between Florence and the sea and to divert it away from the rival city of Pisa.

While working on this scheme he made some remarkable studies,

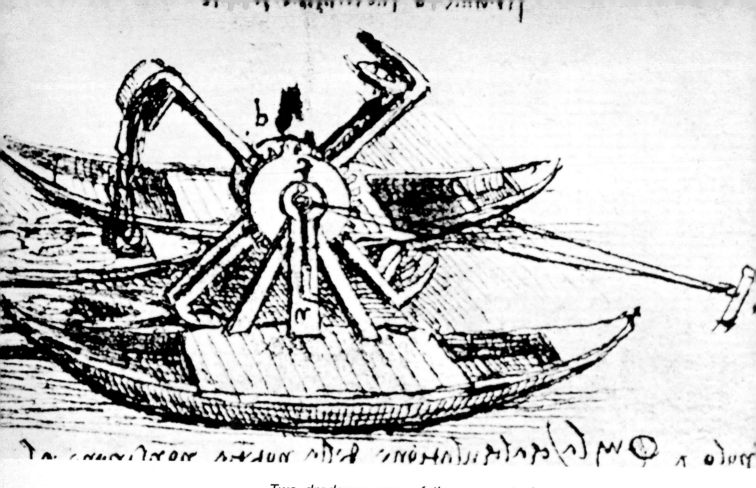

Two dredgers, one of them mounted on pontoons, and the other designed to serve also as a landing berth.

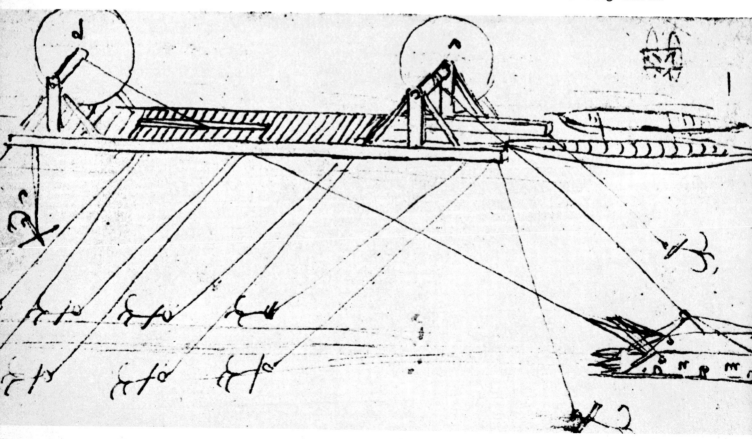

particularly a picture of the Arno basin which is strongly reminiscent of modern cardiology. Locks, waterfalls put to use to provide energy, developed river banks, artificial regulatory lakes – everything was provided for.

He even went so far as to 'tunnel' the course of the river in order to have it cross the Serravalla foothills; astonishingly enough, this same route and the same method was used five hundred years later, by the builders of the divided highway between Florence and the sea!

Another grand idea was the plan for a canal linking Milan to Lake Como, involving a giant lock gate one hundred feet high.

He even proposed to the Venetians the construction of a gigantic dike with sluice-gates which would have made it possible to drown the Turkish army which was stationed down in the plain.

Throughout his life he was passionately interested in such scemes; in fact, even during his exile at Amboise he started work on a number of ideas such as plans to make the Loire and the Cher open to navigation.

It is quite clear that, for ventures such as these, the entire hydraulic arsenal generated by Leonardo's imagination, and scattered over the pages of his notebooks, was well suited.

As one turns the pages on discovers a fabulous exuberance of ideas, ranging from the most sophisticated machine to the strangest kind of gadget.

Canals posed numerous problems involving digging, maintenance and use.

Shovels and muscle power were virtually the only means available for the digging of canals in Leonardo's time. He devised an enormous excavator powered by a winch for speed and regularity of operation. All the details are properly described: tow paths, inspection ladders, cottages for the lock-keepers.

In his drawings we see locks capable of offsetting differences of level for ease of navigation.

The locks have two gates solidly secured to the banks of the canal and accessible by two ladders. They are strangely reminiscent of our modern locks. A more detailed sketch of one of the gates shows the opening built into the base of the gate, which makes it possible to equalize pressures upstream and downstream so that the lock can be opened.

He also made provision for the maintenance of canals: the dredger consisted of a large wheel turning on its axis and mounted on a pontoon between two barges which kept it afloat. The silt thus scooped up from the bottom of the canal was tipped into two barges secured to the floating pontoon.

At another point we see another type of dredger: a sort of giant carpenter's plane scraping the bottom of the canal, drawn by two wheels fixed to a floating floor, itself solidly anchored.

Leonardo's drawings include many sorts of pumps.

Firstly, simple water-wheels: these huge paddle-wheels, which are comparable to those which may still be seen today, were used for irrigation.

Other, more sophisticated models are also to be seen:

Overshot wheels, powered by counterweights and tipping their water into channels.

And also entire elevating systems, lifting the water into huge storage tanks from which it could be distributed by means of a series of scooped ladders, powered by the inevitable toothed wheel.

Leonardo was among the first to harness the formidable power of water. Its point of impact on paddle-wheels released an astonishing amount of energy.

He thus devised a dozen applications of the watermill: to grind grains, power lumber or marble mills and even to spin silk, manufacture gunpowder or power crushing mechanisms for paper pulp.

Giving his creative delirium free rein, Leonardo 'invented' all sorts of crazy ideas which he drew, in many instances, with whimsical strokes of the pen:

A diving suit for exploring the bottom of harbors and the hulls of ships; snorkels; swimmers' gloves for greater power and speed in the water; astonishing floats for walking on water; and even life rafts and lifebelts.

Moreover, he designed an ingenious array of air-filled tanks which could easily be secured to sunken vessels to bring them to the surface.

Above all, his appetite for understanding the laws of the universe drove him to evaluate and control the forces and power which he used.

He studied all natural phenomena emanating from water: humidity, clouds, steam, waves, tides. He invented equipment to measure them and to bring them more completely under control. For the first time in human history the problems of water were beginning to yield to enquiry.

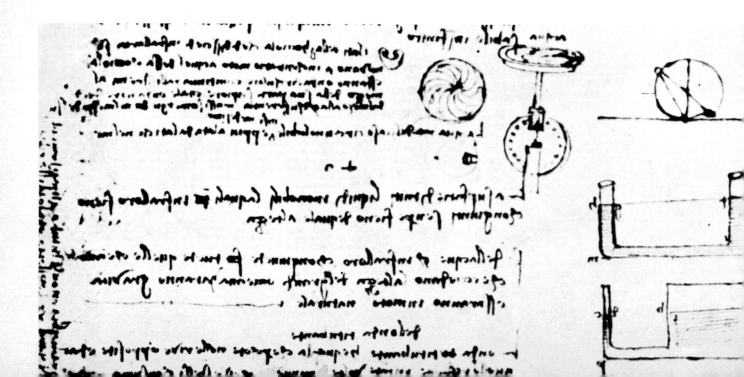

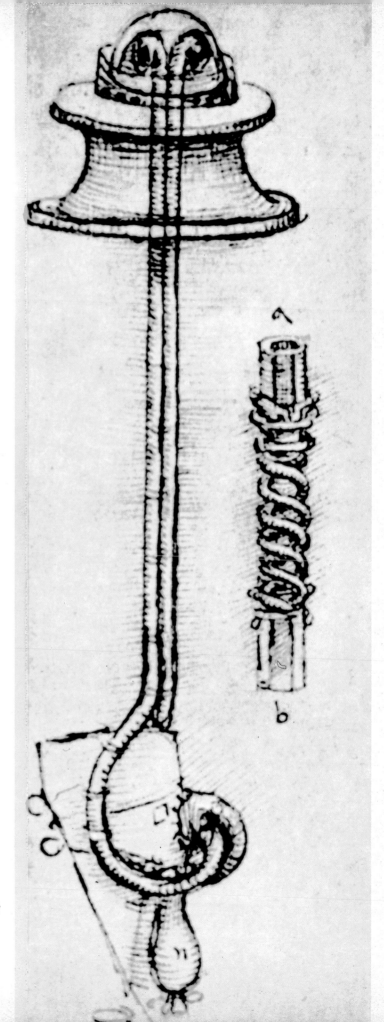

*Left-hand page: advanced studies
of communicating vessels.
Right: snorkel linked to a buoy.*

This page: design for a ship's paddle.
Below, left: similar design in which the paddle is controlled by a handle.
Right: water collector.
Right-hand page:
Facing: this is Leonardo's idea of a diver's suit and... a lifebelt (picture on right).
Middle: equipment which, in his opinion, should have made it possible to walk on water.

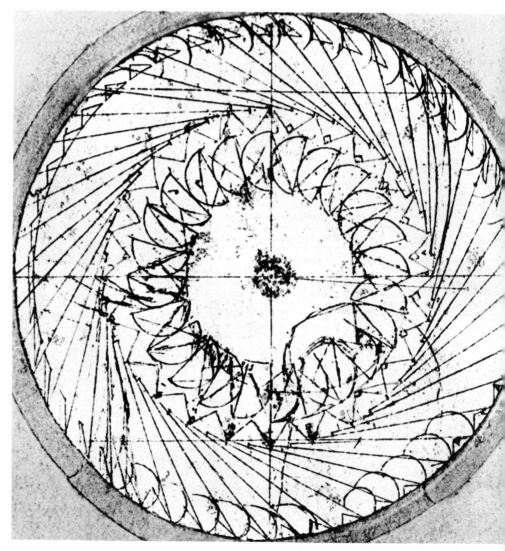

Above: design for a device which, it was hoped, would make it possible to swim on the the waves; technique for breathing under water.

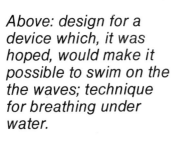

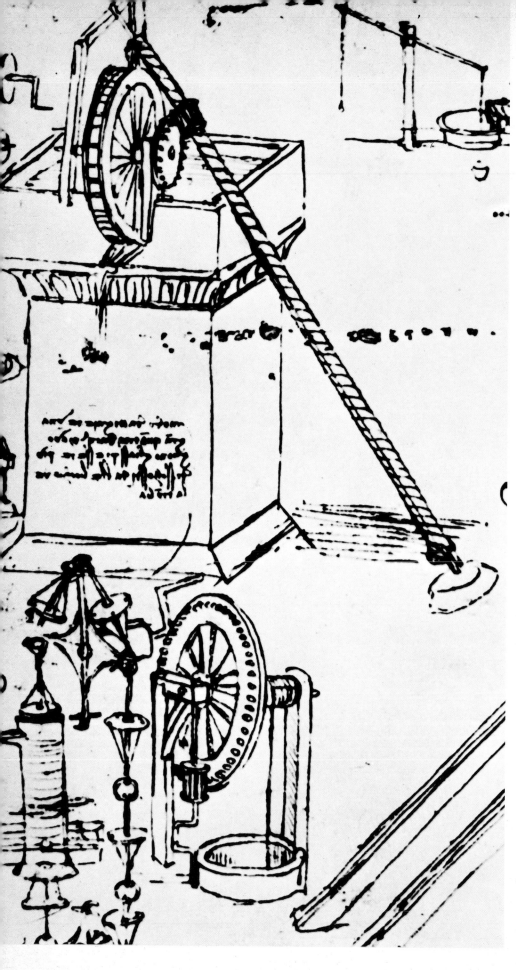

*Left: models of
pumps driven by
chains.
Right: device for the
mechanical collec-
tion of water.*

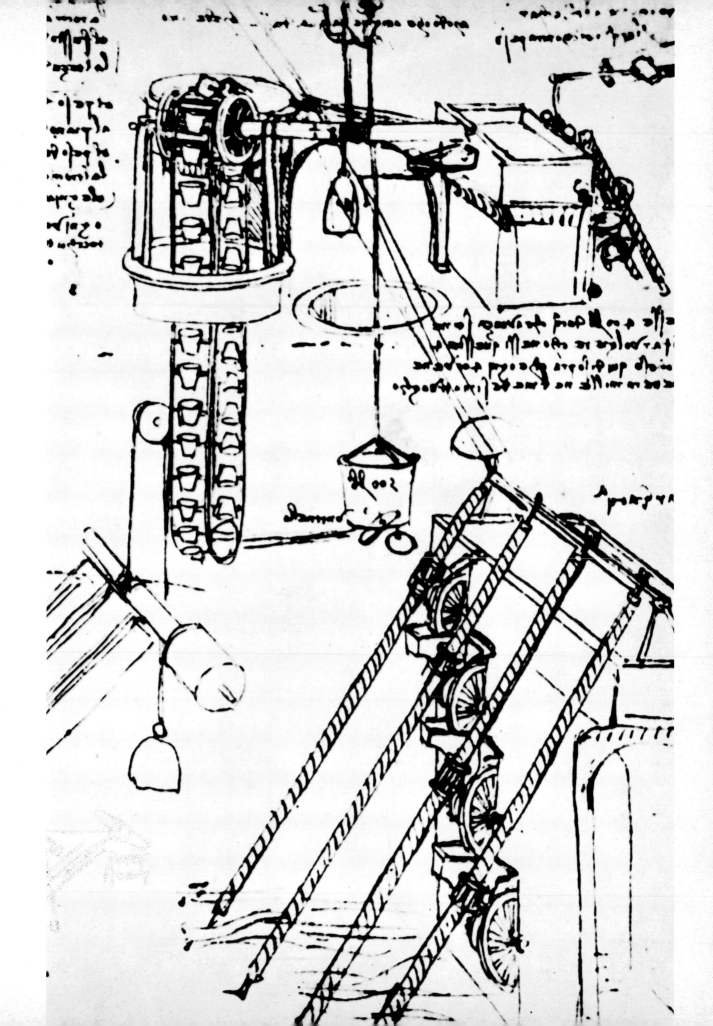

Aeronautics: this is one of the fields in which Leonardo, even today, seems to us to be most astonishing and prophetic.

Yet the idea itself was neither new nor original; indeed much greater inventive genius went into the conception of movement on an apparently irrational two-wheeled bicycle than into the realization of the ancient dream of Icarus.

Flight had always been an ambition of man; and the adventure of Icarus, who escaped from the Cretan labyrinth by means of a pair of wings attached to his body, seems highly symbolic of that forlorn hope.

One should not forget, however, than in the 15th century, despite the extremely lively state of Renaissance scientific research, none of the fundamental notions of aerostatics, aerodynamics and aeronautics – the technical basis of light – were known.

Through the notion of the resistance of the air, which had been noticed and understood by Leonardo, research had come to recognize 'lift' as an essential part of the quest, but had gone no further.

Leonardo's research was thus lacking in neither courage nor boldness; indeed it posed a challenge to the thinking of his day.

We should not forget that it was not until 1783, at Annonay in France, that the first hot-air balloon rose from the ground, though the principles on which it was based had been used, in other circumstances, by Leonardo.

It was not until 1890 that the first 'aircraft' made its appearance, solving for the first time the problem of heavier-than-air flight.

Those four centuries of fruitless research make Leonardo's failures seem much less significant, leaving one aware only of the obstinacy of his efforts and the prophetic genius of his ingenious and visionary solutions.

Ever since his childhood in Tuscany he had been fascinated by the flight of birds in the hills. Their movements, combining gracefulness with agility and efficiency had nurtured his thinking about natural history, in which he blended a fondness for scientific observation and the sensory poetry of shapes.

These memories gave rise to his first intellectual efforts when, having exhausted the problems of water, he then decided to turn his attention to those of the air.

It was during his second stay in Milan and his second Florentine period that he made his first sketches and wrote his first notes on this new subject, in which he was so far ahead of his times.

It seemed obvious to him from the outset that the solution to his problem was to be found in the flight of birds. It seemed logical to attempt to unlock the fabulous mystery of the bird's wing in order to transpose it to the mechanical sphere.

The analysis and recording of all the phases of winged flight really required an eye such as his – fast, accurate and long accustomed to all aspects of the observation of nature.

The drawings which represent them are extraordinary: front view, profile, three quarters view, all positions and postures are analyzed, dismantled and then reproduced. This fantastic strip cartoon comes alive and lives, superb in both its poetry and its accuracy, just like a series of photographs recording each moment of the flapping of a bird's wings.

Gradually, by a graphic study of these positions, he transformed them into mechanical patterns, shifting from the fresco of the painter to the industrial design of the engineer.

Though technically perfect, his work was based on wrong ideas. Yet, for a quarter of a century Leonardo was to persist stubbornly in building mechanical wings copied from those of the bat, which he regarded as the essential basis of any flying machine.

He never lost heart, in spite of repeated failures.

One wonders, in fact, whether he was really aware of his failures. It is thought that he must have conducted actual tests during which he must have realized that his machines would never be able to take off.

But it is also possible that he may have been content to design increasingly complex and sophisticated machines, merely for the pleasure of accumulating the greatest possible number of solutions: admirable dreams, superb inventions serving no purpose at all.

First we see mechanical translations directly deriving from observation of living things, astonishing assemblies of jointed ribs and mobile cranks – all strongly reminiscent of a dissection of puppets moved by cables and levers.

Here we find a perfect reflection of Leonardo's characteristic style which provides us with an ideal illustration of the workings of his mind and his scientific approach. In this way, on the basis of the schematized analysis of the tendons of the hand, he designed his ingenious clarinet keys; or adapted a caricature of the larynx and the trachea in the design of flutes which reproduce the human anatomy in stylized form.

This time he transposes the bird's wing into mechanical architectonics. When the structure was completed he made sure that it could be set in motion by human muscular effort.

The most significant of his sketches is undoubtedly a remarkably lifelike giant bat-wing, powered by a man pulling on an enormous lever. That wing was clearly intended for the study of the flapping motions thus obtained, probably to compare them with those of a real wing.

Once the wing was transposed to a mechanical structure and its dynamic features deemed to be correct, it was necessary to include the driving force which was of crucial importance in any design for a flying machine. It is at this point that the succession of drawings strike the modern reader as both absurd and inspired; they also clearly call to mind 19th-century illustrations of science fiction. They closely resemble the astonishing yet practical flying machines drawn by Jules Verne, for example, in *Robur the Conqueror.*

The remarkable thing is that, throughout a whole series of drawings, Leonardo seems concerned only with the flapping mechanism, while totally neglecting the truly essential problem of the 'motor' of his machines.

Sometimes he goes so far as to show only the essential mechanical organs or some specific detail of an invention, often in an enlarged view.

These might show, for example, a vertical axis operating a pair of paddles designed to flap with a reciprocal rising motion; or a complex 'motor unit' consisting of two pulleys fitted with a belt ending in a pair of stirrups, operated by the hands or feet of the pilot, which drive four paddles simulating a symbolic flapping of wings.

More interesting, however, are the complete flying machines which Leonardo designed. In these drawings the artist rises above mere technical detail and sets forth his dreams and visions, in which poetic delirium overshadows mechanical plausibility. It is almost as if, tiring of his hopeless task, Leonardo's creative genius suddenly became aware of the impotence of current technology and left the field free for his imagination.

The reader is occasionally startled by strange new variations on the basic ornithopter theme: a new king of airborne skiff, whose pilot was supposed to lie stretched out in order to use the oars which pulled against the air instead of the water; or the astonishing craft which has its flying mechanism supported severaly yards above the ground on crutches and a ladder: once the long-awaited take-off had actually occurred, the crutches and ladder would be mechanically folded – the first retractable undercarriage in the history of aviation.

However, it was essential to come back to earth and tackle the real problem: propulsion, and, in particular, the total lock of boost capable of achieving a take-off.

The pitiable muscle-power of man could clearly not be expected to provide a solution.

Indeed, Leonardo must have been aware of the pathetically limited capacity of human muscle, the only driving force available to him.

No matter how many devious mechanical contrivances he used, performing prodigious feats of reduction and transmission, all he succeeded in doing was increasing the weight of the machine by adding more and more gears and levers – a particularly grave handicap when one remembers the kind of materials available at the time.

The only way to get these 'heavier-than-air' machines off the ground was to use a powerful form of propulsion which simply did not exist at the time.

In the circumstances, then, what is one to think of the sketches of 'pilots' which occur from time to time in Leonardo's notebooks? Did he really believe that the man who is shown moving a lever operating a set of ludicrous paddles was actually going to take off in his machine? Did he think that the four hapless individuals who are pedalling furiously, suspended under a 'flying wing', were going to lift it above the ground? Could he have hoped that the two convicts, strapped to the enormous wheel which they were supposed to turn like squirrels in a cage, were really going to take their craft aloft?

And what can one possibly say about the pilot, enclosed in his perfectly astonishing machine shaped like a cup on two ladders, whose superhuman task is to become airborne by beating the air with two pairs of oars?

It seems to us unthinkable that Leonardo could have been so deluded and could have failed to realize that there could be no question of biceps or calf muscles generating enough power to overcome

Pedal-powered wing...

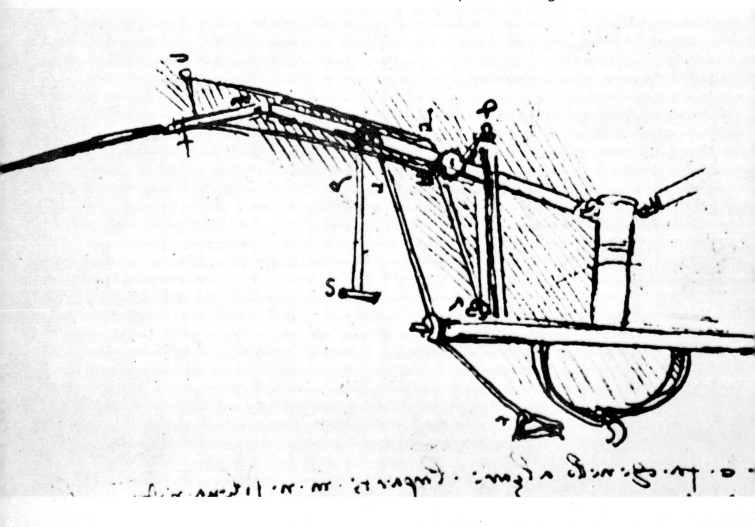

the relentless effects of gravity.

In our opinion he was so sure of the truth that he suddenly steered his research in a new direction.

Finding it impossible to leave the ground by means of the flapping or artificial wings, he thereafter decided to concentrate on the study of the air's own 'lift' capacity.

Basing his deductions on the analysis of the gliding flights of birds and the motion of falling leaves, he determined and measured the aerodynamic components of the air; he even invented instruments in order to better assess them: the first anemometers, barometers and inclinometers of aeronautic history.

Then, drawing on the new data provided by his observations, he did work which was centuries ahead of his time, accurately foreseeing the possibilities of the glider, the hang-glider and the parachute.

One of his famous drawings, which is caricatural but suggestive, clearly shows a man hanging from a strange pyramid-shaped parachute which, though unconventional by modern standars, is doubtless functional.

The fuselage of what could be a flying machine.

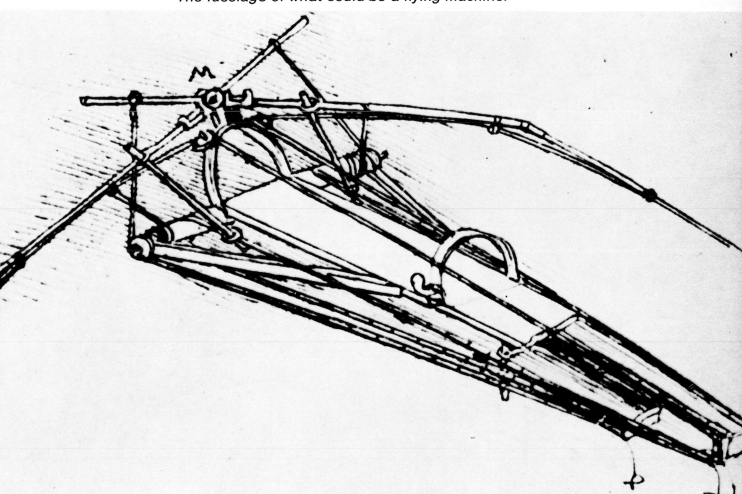

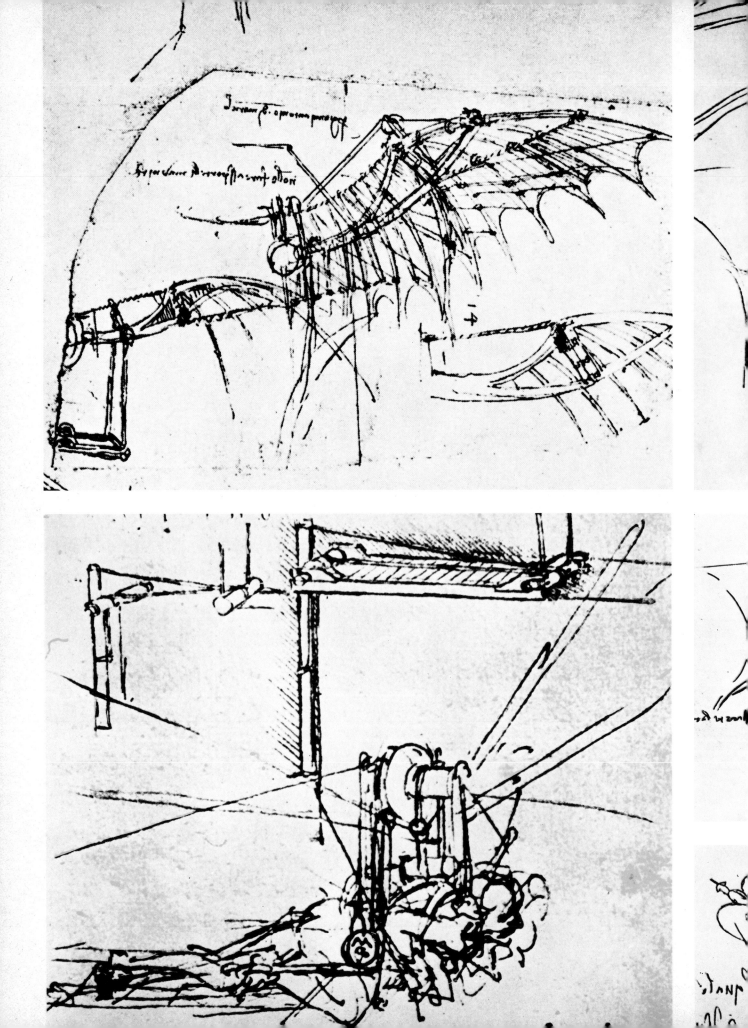

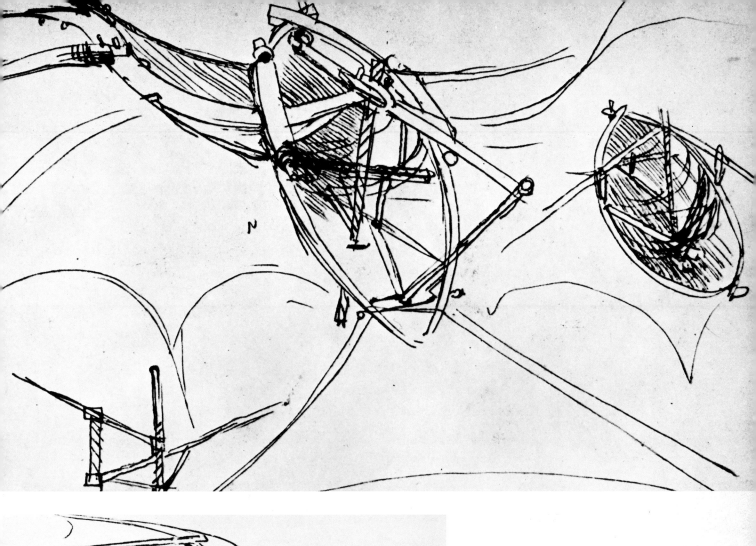

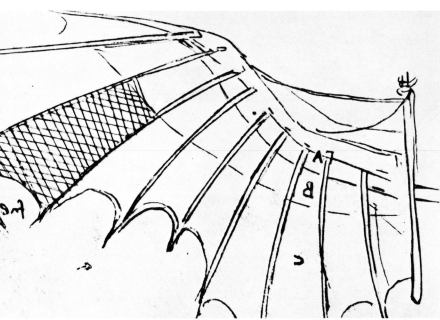

Top left: studies for the covered wing of a flying machine.
Above: manually driven flying machine.
Bottom left: design for a foot-powered wing moving mechanism.
Facing: design for a wing with cloth-covered controls.
Below, left: here Leonardo has made a note on the flight of birds, wondering how they are able to take off in perfectly still air. Right: detail of bird feathers.

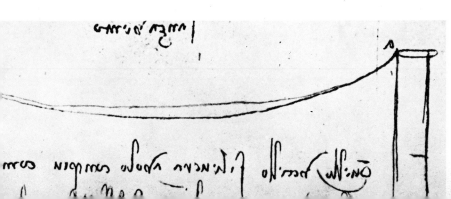

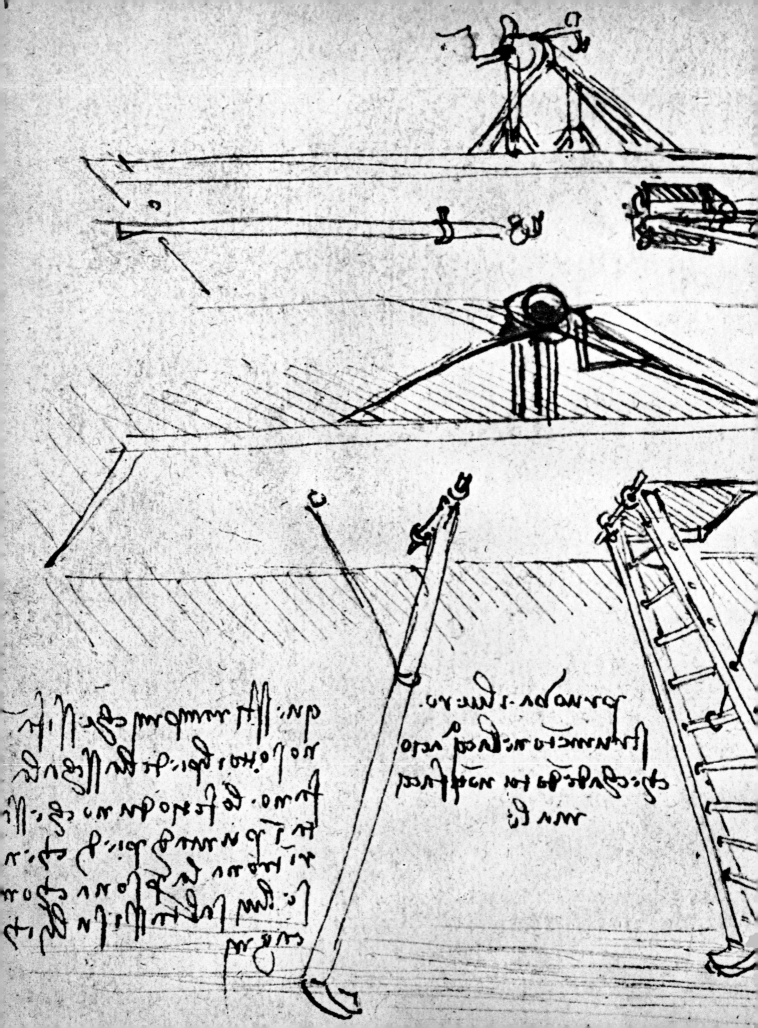

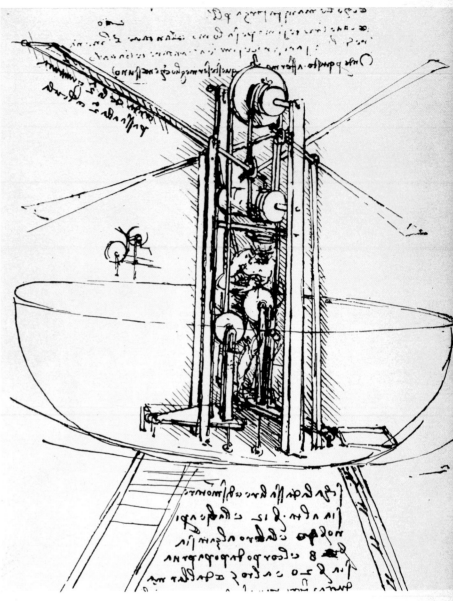

Left: design for a manually operated flying machine with an undercarriage.
Above: design for flying machine with room for a person to stand up.

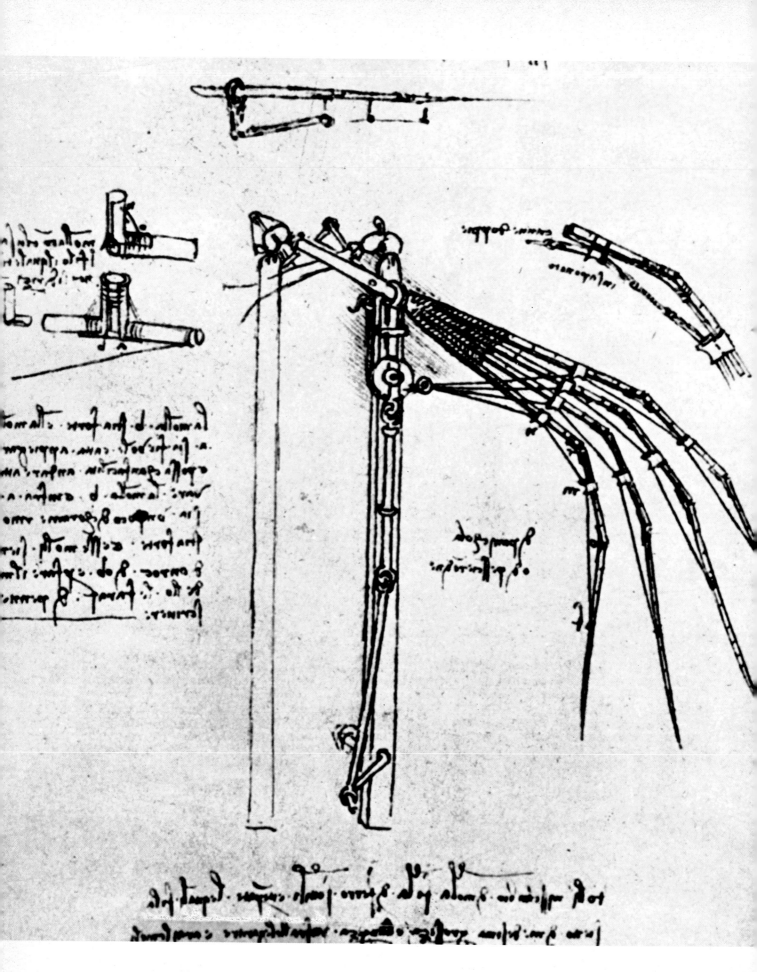

This was because Leonardo, though unable to resolve the problem of propulsion which is crucial for take-off, had a full mastery of the theories of 'lift', which he had already anticipated and used in his hydraulic and ballistic experiments.

So it was that, deliberately leaving aside the insoluble problem of propulsion, he designed and drew what must surely be his most prophetic vision of all: his design for an aerial screw.

The two super-imposed disks, driven by a mysterious rotary mechanism, are nothing other than an early form of the helicopter.

There can be no doubt that Leonardo's aeronautical failures were due to the lack of an autonomous energy supply which effectively ruled out real mechanical progress in his period.

With our modern energy sources at his disposal, however, he would clearly have come very close, in this entirely new field of aerial locomotion, to the solutions which were eventually adopted four centuries later.

He would soon have dropped the romantic myth of reproducing the flight of birds, and concentrated wholly on the immense potential of propulsion and lift combined.

Eventually, whether through disillusionment or a return to reason, he started jotting down in his notebooks some conventional but highly effective outlines of windmills, using the force of the wind which had flouted him all along.

Perhaps they are the symbol of a glorious defeat which enabled Leonardo/Jules Verne the visionary to join in legend Leonardo/Don Quichotte the lyrical poet.

Left: design for a wing with a spring.
Right: note on the way birds' feathers are assembled.

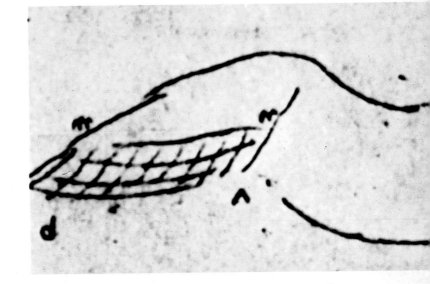

40

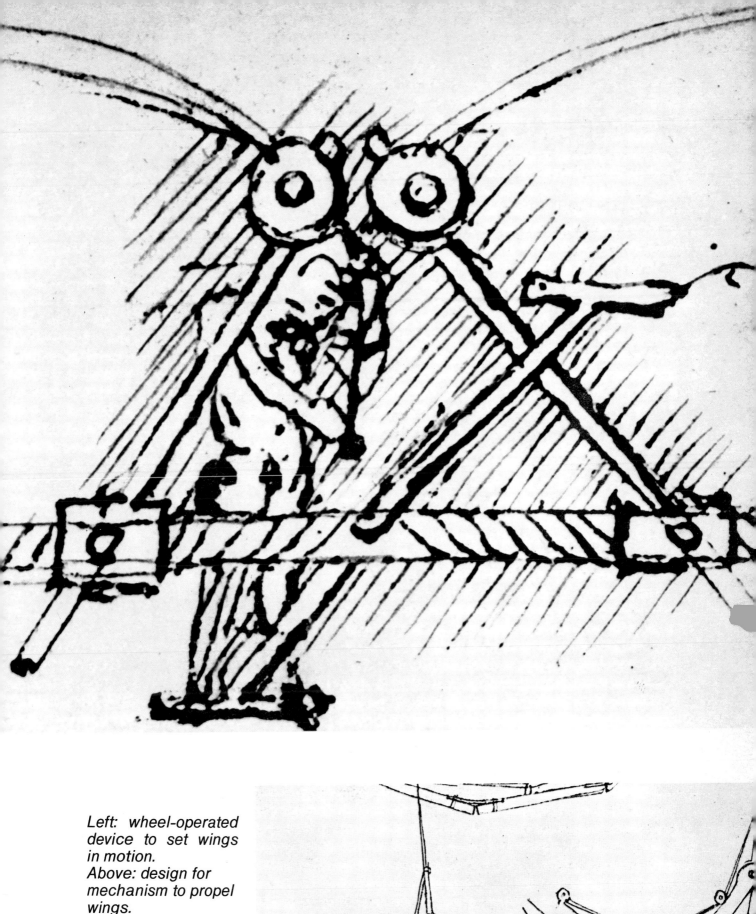

Left: wheel-operated device to set wings in motion.
Above: design for mechanism to propel wings.
Right: how to unfold wings.

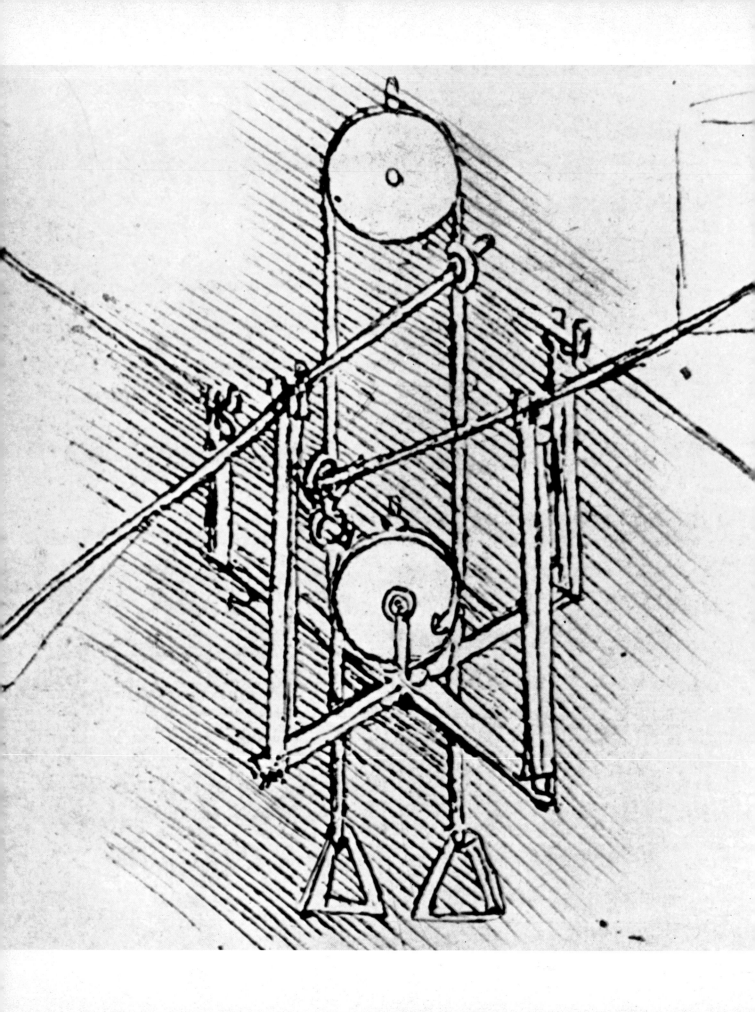

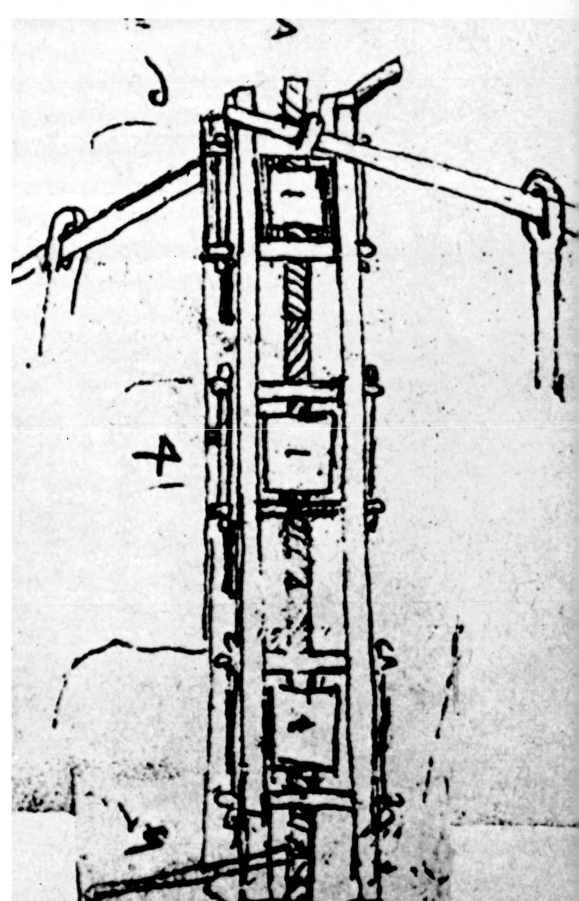

Left: design for a pulley-driven power plant. Right: a similar device, only this time driven by a spiral screw.

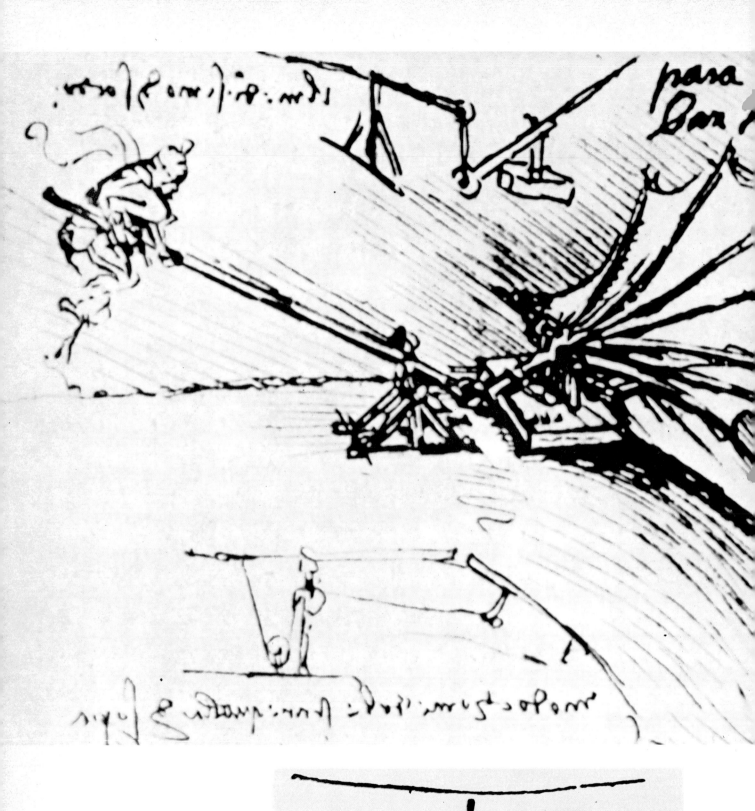

Above: details of an experiment to determine the aerodynamic forces applied to the wing. Facing: position of the pilot of a flying machine.

Above and facing: Leonardo imagined that it was safe to jump into the void if one was weering a hermetically sealed canvas parachute measuring 58 feet by 58 feet.

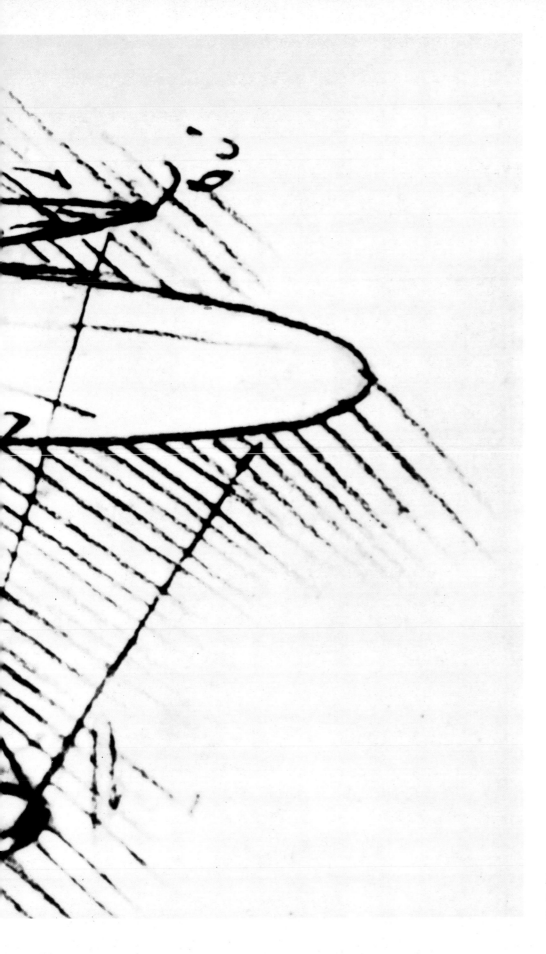

*Another device con-
ceived by Leonardo:
a sort of helicopter.*

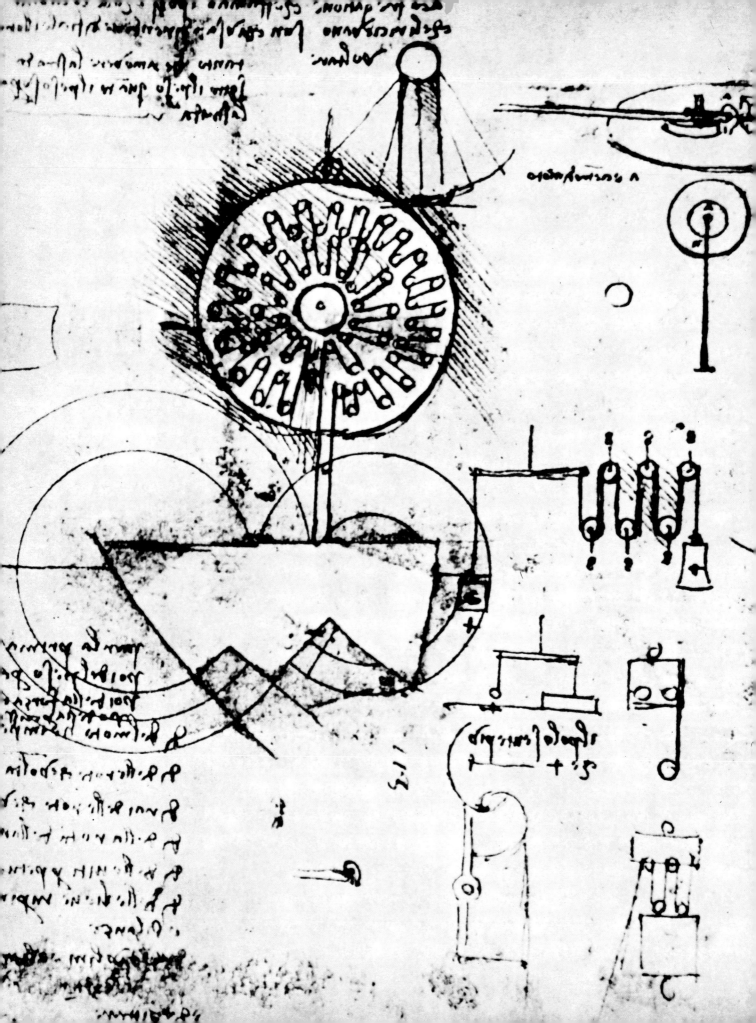

« Mechanics is a paradise for mathematicians. » This remark of Leonardo's explains why he gave such a privileged place to technology considered as the practical application of abstract theories.

For him mechanical invention was the art of the concrete, confronting the human values of mathematical speculation with pragmatic reality.

Yet even before creating the famous 'machines' which were to be the transposition to the engineering level of the fantasies of a scientific mind, he sought to materialize each law and each principle of general physics.

In this way he arrived at a large number of 'elements of mechanics' – simple tools emanating directly from scientific observations and forming part of 'machines', just as ingredients are used in a recipe.

On page after page of his notebooks one sees the materialization of these mechanical elements, in graphic form: screws, pins, winches, pulleys, joints, springs, paddles, gears, levers, chains, pistons, toothed wheels, pinions and other aspects of the world of mechanics. Sometimes they are given several interpretations: there are, for example, sixty-seven different crank mechanisms for converting reciprocating to rotary motion, and *vice versa.*

Having been thus studied, drawn and designed, they were promptly applied to the solution of general mechanical problems involved in making the most complex machines.

Processes for hoisting and the transmission of motion lie at the basis of each study. Leonardo was particularly fascinated by two points: the conversion of reciprocal to rotary motion, and *vice versa,* on the one hand; and the use of reducing gears in order to keep on infinitely adding to the power of the force applied.

Having a mastery of these essential elements of general mechanics, he could launch into his sometimes rather wild dreams as a visionary, and often prophetic, engineer.

Early on, however, he perceived one of his limits: the inadequacy of the energy sources of his period. He was even moved to look for others, such as steam.

What, one wonders, might such a man have invented if he had had all our modern energy resources at his disposal?

His rendering of these basic mechanical components is astonishingly precise: the links of his chains are identical to those of our modern bicycles; his automatic release hooks could well have been taken from a modern catalogue. He even devised ball bearings, including a conical pivot with three balls which was 'reinvented' in 1920, as well as a disk bearing system which is strongly reminiscent of our contemporary clutch mechanisms.

Through his pen the tools of his period are transformed and evolve. He gave both peasant and worker tools to make their work more comfortable and more productive.

Essentially, Leonardo the engineer was the true father of the machine tool.

Yet he did not allow his work to drift. Renaissance Italy, in particular Florence and Milan, were alive with the efforts of craftsmen to whom they owed their prosperity. Theirs, however, was a traditional type of activity, based on painfully slow techniques.

It was in order to increase 'profitability', as we would say today, that Leonardo tried to use automation as a way of transforming the ancestral operations of his day, bringing them into a truly industrial phase.

It seems surprising, therefore, that most of these projects remained in the stage of sketches; almost all of them, though perfectly feasible and economically attractive, were in fact 'rediscovered' several centuries later.

This sterility and his failure to complete his work had much to do with Leonardo's character. He was curious about all problems facing scientists and engineers, but was really interested only in their solution, and abandoned them as soon as he had, if only in a sketch, understood and resolved them.

Despite the intense shortage of money which harassed him throughout his life, he never sought to make his machines functional so as to derive a well-earned financial advantage for himself.

Some of them were actually so efficient that, when they saw the light of day in the 18th and 19th centuries, their yield posed such a threat to traditional manual techniques that they evoked the first wave of enthusiasm and the first social conflicts of the Industrial Revolution.

It is in his drawings of these prophetic machines that Leonardo strikes us as the sublime precursor of industrial designers. He used a pen, so as to be able to pass easily from the sketch to the notes which explained it. His drawings combine great accuracy and technical thoroughness with the beauty of a work of art, as can be seen from their superb balance and composition and the confident elegance of the pen-strokes; sometimes, in a nice esthetic flourish, the drawing is underlined with a brown or ochre wash-tint.

It has been possible, as is well known, to build perfect working models from these drawings. The modern Italian engineers who made his hopes a reality noticed, in the process, that there were too many, or too few, springs, pins or cogs, in certain designs.

When one considers the absolute precision of the sketches, which

Right: release mechanism and design for a traveling crane.

50

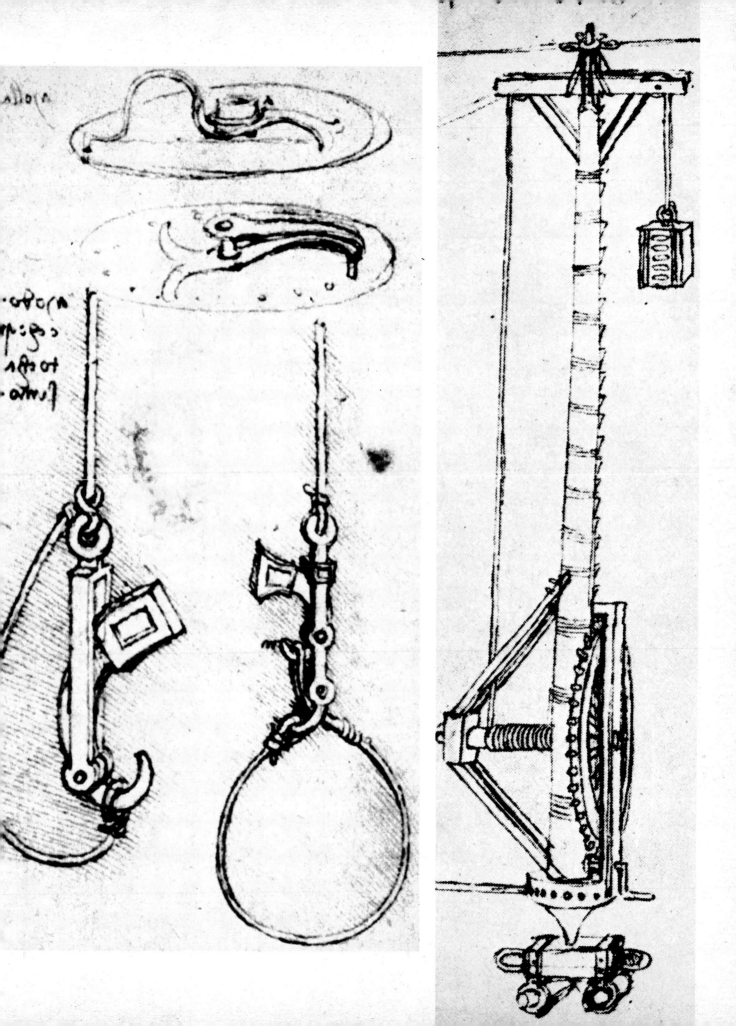

show the finest details, it is unlikely that these irregularities were due to mistakes or carelessness.

Perhaps these 'flaws' were deliberate? Rather like the 'mirror' handwriting which he used in his notes, may be they were slipped into the finished drawing so as to deter plagiarists, by making them harder to understand and more mysterious. This may well have been a naive form of scientific paternity seeking protection against hypothetical industrial espionage.

Leonardo's machine tools are so numerous that one has to choose the more original amongst them or those with the most interesting practical applications.

The file-cutting machine (1480) was Leonardo's first invention. Before his time the rasps and files used in carpentry and metalworking had been made by hand with hammer and graver. Each unit of the machine consisted of a graving hammer powered by a toothed wheel turned by a counterweight. With each rotation it dropped onto the file, while moved forward at the same pace. A combination of six units mounted in series made it possible to achieve a high output.

It was not until the beginning of the twentieth century that this process was eventually adopted. The same principle was also applied by Leonardo to the design of a machine for stamping strips of gold or tin as they emerged from a rolling-mill.

The development of mechanical engineering made it essential to develop processes for the rapid machining of certain parts.

In the sketch the cylinder which is to be bored is held solidly in a vertical position by machine-vices, in the axis of a polisher consisting of a grooved drum covered with an abrasive mixture of oil and emery powder. When driven with a helicoidal motion, the drum spreads the abrasive and constantly rubs the surfaces to be polished.

Leonardo designed many types of rolling-mill, in the broad sense of the term, to stretch or flatten the various metals used in the industries of his day.

For rolling into strips or sheets, he passed the metals between two heavy pressure cylinders.

In order to stretch them into wire or fine strips, he applied enormous traction power by means of large sets of reducing gears.

In all cases, the use of technical innovations such as the ball bearing and a free wheel ratchet system for levers and handles made work much easier and reduced to the minimum losses of power due to excess friction.

Tin, copper, iron and even the precious metals could be treated in this way.

The considerable development of the craft of weaving, the pride of the rich cities of the Italian Renaissance, led Leonardo to seek ways of automating the preparatory and manufacturing phases of this industry, which was in the hands of artists.

He designed a *rope making machine;* a proper *spinning machine:* the use of reciprocal motion made it possible to wind thread evenly on

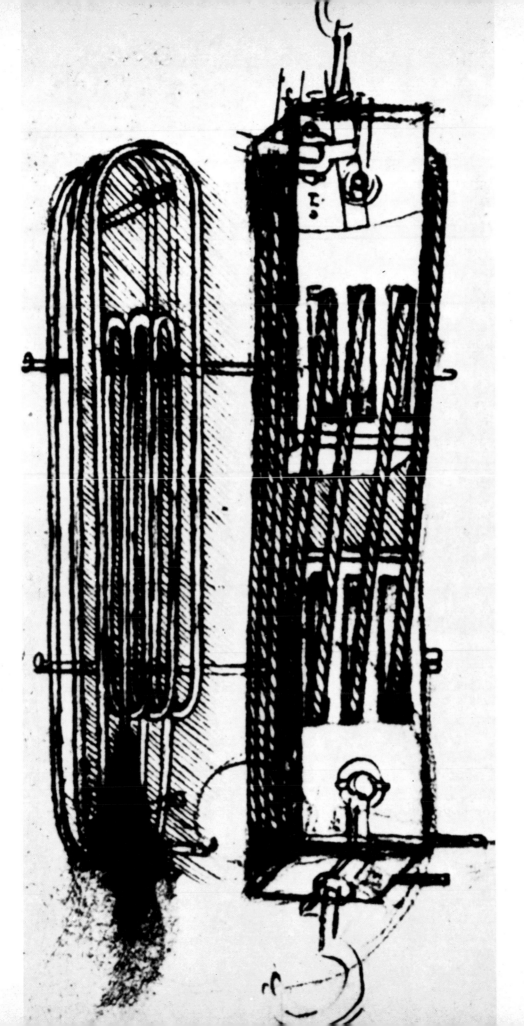

Pulley for use in testing the resistance of rigging.

the entire distaff through the use of a pendulum spindle.

Of particular note is his *fabric stretcher:* the fabric, stretched on a wooden frame, was automatically cut by two huge shears. As in most of these inventions the coupling of several units made it possible to achieve an almost industrial level of output. When this machine was re-invented in England in the 18th century, replacing the workers who had previously performed these tasks, grave social conflicts ensued as the employment of large numbers of workers was threatened.

Inversely, there is a sketch of a *'wool-maker':* an instrument which could artificially fluff up high-quality fabrics which had been woven smooth.

Using an optical principle, Leonardo even devised a way of increasing the luminosity of oil lamps by passing their light through a glass bowl full of water, which produced a magnifying effect. European lace-makers used this method empirically several centuries later.

His woodworking tools included *planes* for wood held in a vice; also, particularly, *drills* since the plumbing of the period was made of tree trunks hollowed out by hand: the log, securely held along the axis by steel jaws, was hollowed out in the form of a regular cylinder by an immense drill bit towards which it was gradually drawn by a weight and a set of reducing gears.

Together with the conversion of rotary to reciprocal motion, and *vice versa,* the design of hoisting equipment was the one field of applied physics which most excited Leonardo. In fact he produced dozens of different versions of such devices.

Windlasses, cranes, winches and pulley-blocks are strewn throughout the pages of his notebooks – each seeking, through sophisticated reducing gears, to outdo all the others in efficiency. The one we have chosen is among the most perfect and precise designs of which working models have been built in modern times. It used the reciprocal motion of a lever, converting it to rotary motion to roll a traction cable on an arc. A ratchet system prevented backwards motion, and a reducing gear yielded enormous power which a child could control with a simple gesture.

The invention of an automatic release mechanism greatly facilitated the lifting of heavy loads. Mounted as a pivot on a stirrup, the release mechanism was equipped with a counterweight; the pull of the load held the cable taut, but, as soon as the load touched the ground, causing the cable to slacken, the counterweight pivoted and released the hook.

This list is merely a sampling of the revolutionary ideas of Leonardo. Each album of sketches contains dozens of others: a machine for sharpening needles by means of leather straps (Leonardo hoped that it would bring him a profit of 16,000 ducats!). A machine for making evenly threaded metallic screws; machines for automatically resetting the newly invented printed presses, for which Italy was one of the major European centers.

His attention was even drawn by the power system for roasting

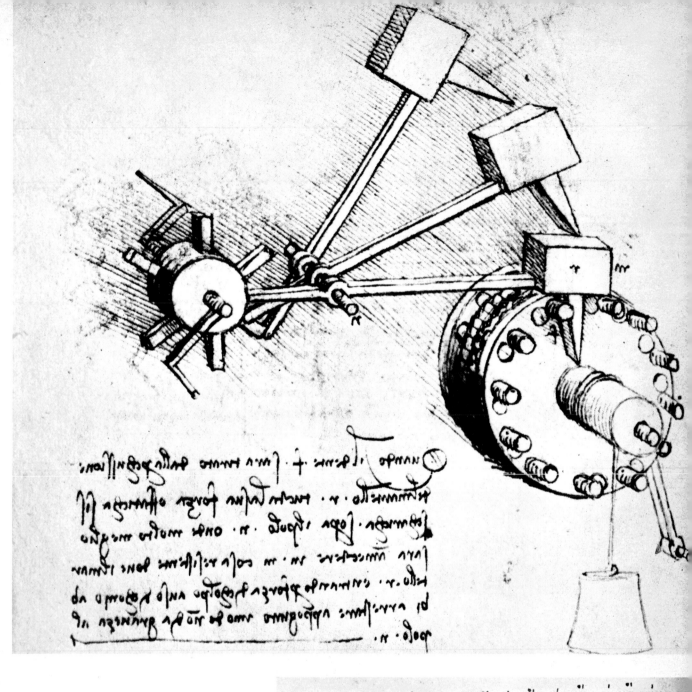

Above: Leonardo intended this set
of gears to control a counterweight.
Facing: transmission wheels, with
brake.

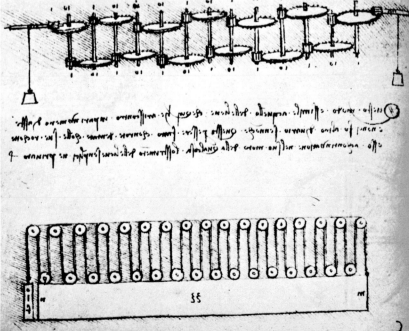

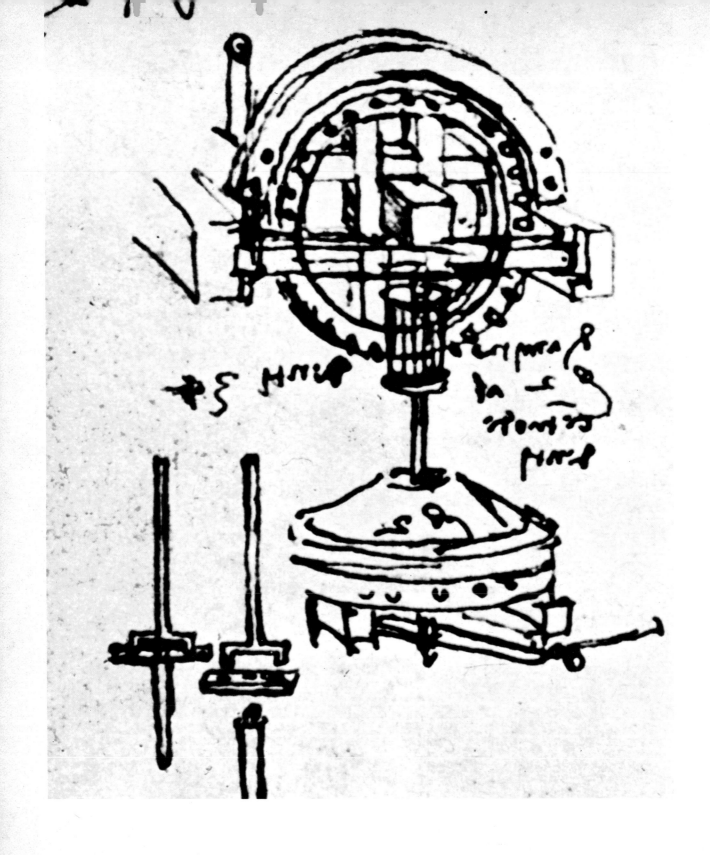

Above: transmission wheel and brake. Right, top: detail of jointed chains. Bottom: multiple capacity transmission axle. (shaft).

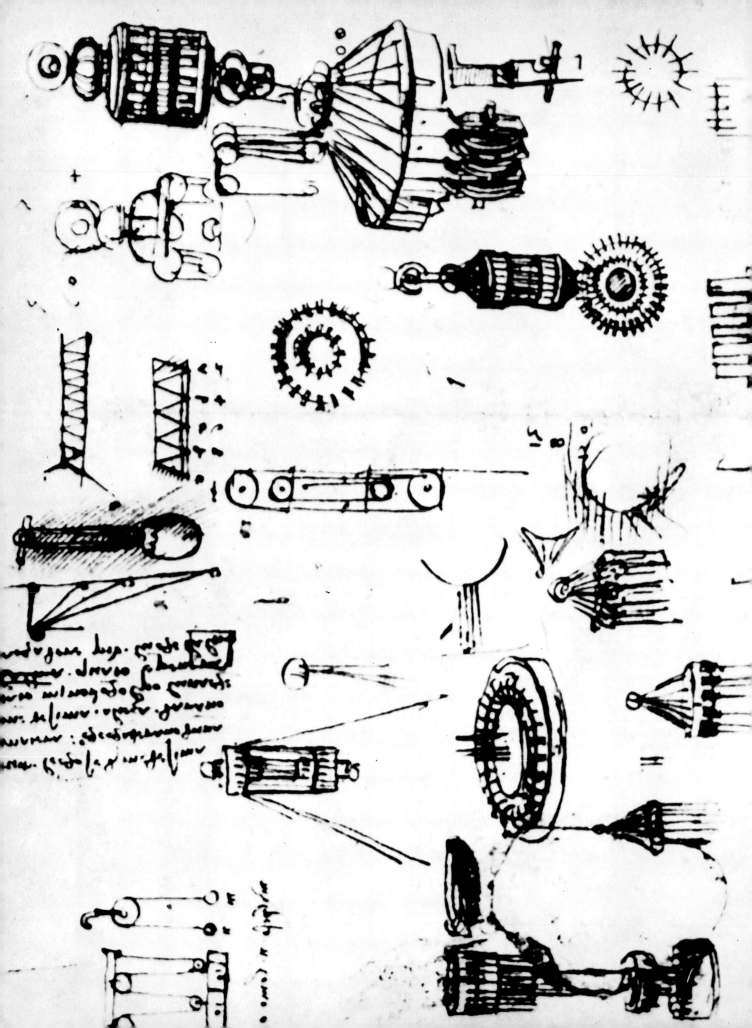

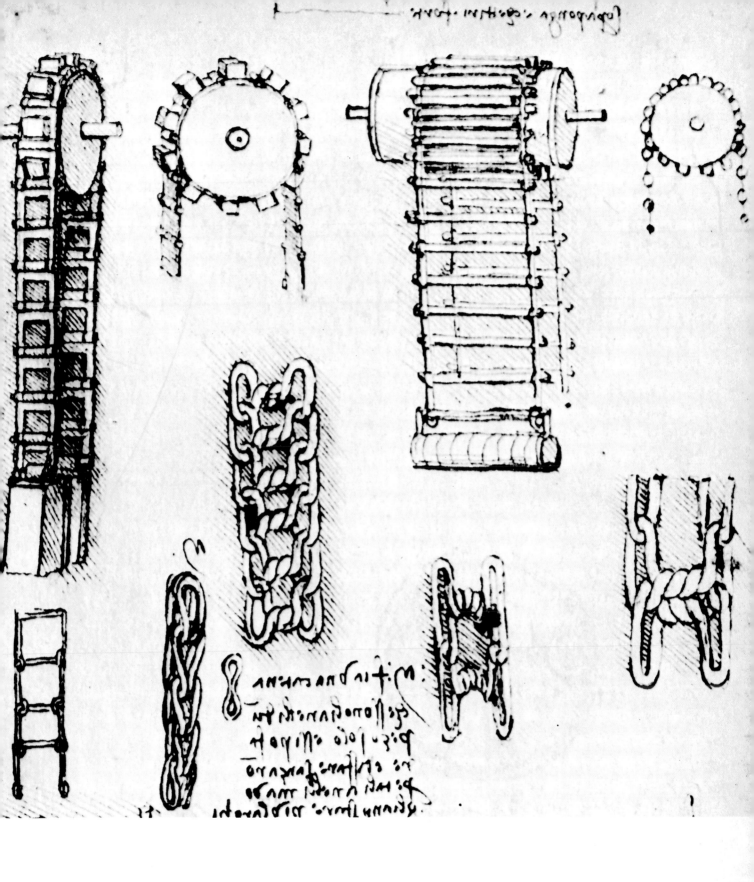

*Left: studies for a pulley-block
and (above) transmission chains.*

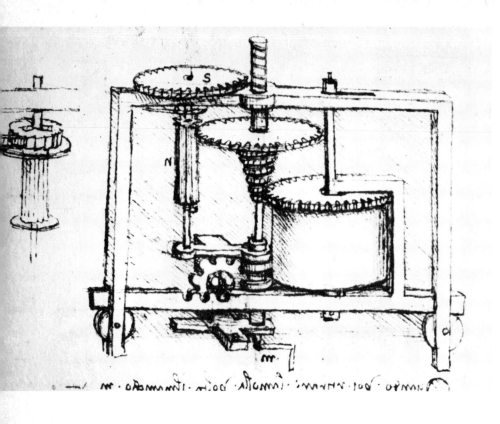

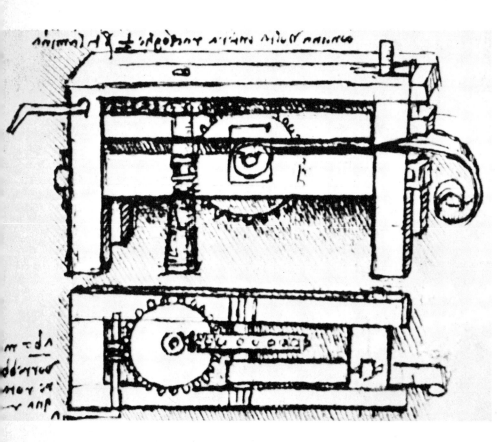

Left-hand pagee: cog-wheels.
Facing: motor with gear-wheels.
Bottom: rolling mill for lead and copper.

spits. Besides a conventional model powered by a weight, a much fancier type harnessed the force of rising hot air to drive an airscrew which turned the spit. This technique had the advantage, as he himself notes, of being adjustable: the hotter the fire, the faster the rotation of the blades, and, accordingly, of the roast!

The ultimate, masterly touch of this restless search for new ideas was Leonardo's automatically closing toilet seat!

Since he had none of our modern sources of energy, Leonardo had to rely on exclusively mechanical methods for generating motion.

He devised a curious *car* – actually a simple platform on four wheels – driven by the successive release of several coiled springs powering a set of gears. When one of the springs was being released, the 'driver' had to wind up another, thus obtaining, at least in theory, a smooth motion. When one remembers, however, that the operator, besides controlling the springs, had to steer the vehicle with a fifth small rudder-wheel, it becomes clear that the propulsion of such a prototype would have required an enormous outlay of muscular energy.

His design of the first *bicycle,* on the other hand, was much simpler and more rational. Looking strikingly like our modern models, it was made of wood, with a handlebar, pedals and rear chain drive. The fact of his having thought up such a vehicle, moving balanced on two wheels, clearly demonstrates the amazing creative power of his imagination, in which he rivals the prophetic qualities of the work of Jules Verne.

Leonardo's interest in everything related to measurement naturally led him to turn his attention to the measurement of time.

His mastery of complex systems of gears, springs and counterweights took him into this almost infinite field of mechanical endeavor.

Sand-timers, sundials and sophisticated mechanisms, applicable to both clocks and automatic devices in general, flourished on the pages of his notebooks.

Not only did he draw, for purposes of analysis, all the organs of the clocks of his day, but he improved them by his meticulous quest for greater precision and regularity of movement.

To do this he invented pivots made of semi-precious stones, and even diamonds, in order to reduce friction; he improved the cutting of teeth and cogs; he designed a control system to achieve regularity, regardless of the tension of the spring or the swing of the pendulum.

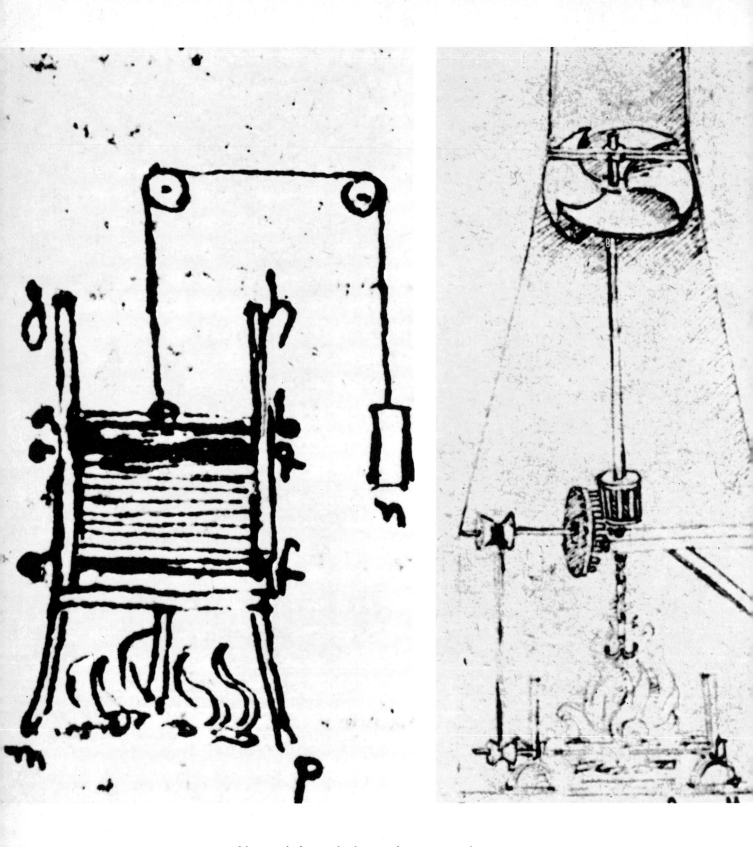

Above, left: techniques for measuring water vapors.
Right: spit-roaster operated by a bellows.
Right-hand page: experts differ as to the proper interpretation
of these illustrations; some feel that it must be a sketch for a
cylinder-based printing system.

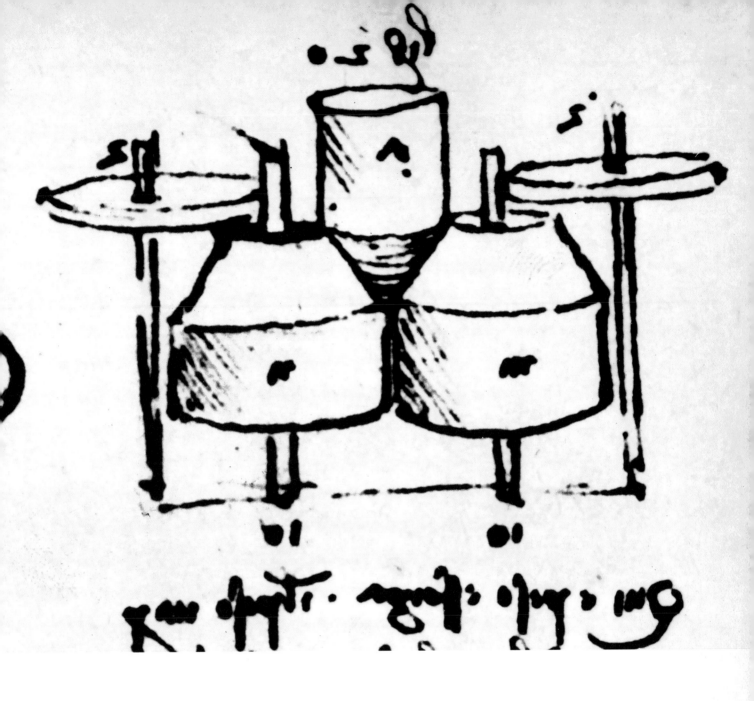

All these accomplishments enabled him to make, rather than merely plan, a number of mechanical toys, some of which were gigantic; for example, the automatic lion, made shortly before his death, for a celebration at the court of Francis I: the lion moved towards the king and opened its breast to discharge an armful of lilies.

One of his inventions which was actually put to use during his last stay at Amboise was a particularly original alarm clock, a kind of liquid sand-timer: water was made to flow in an extremely fine stream from one receptacle to another, and when the lower receptacle was full it weighed down on a lever, the force of which, amplified by means of gears, raised Leonardo's feet suddenly into the air!

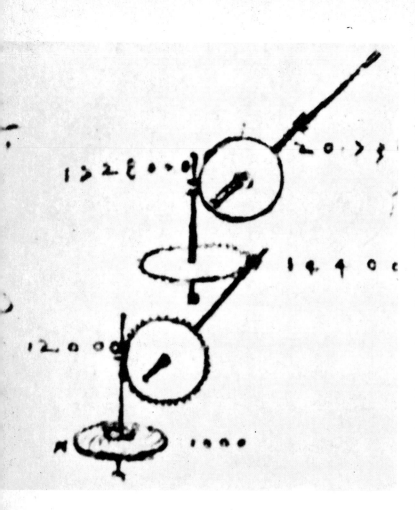

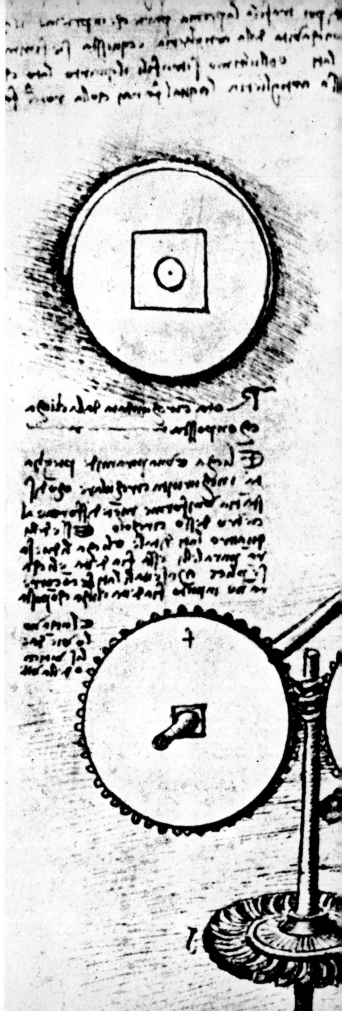

These two pages show designs for a rope-making machine powered by a hydraulic wheel.

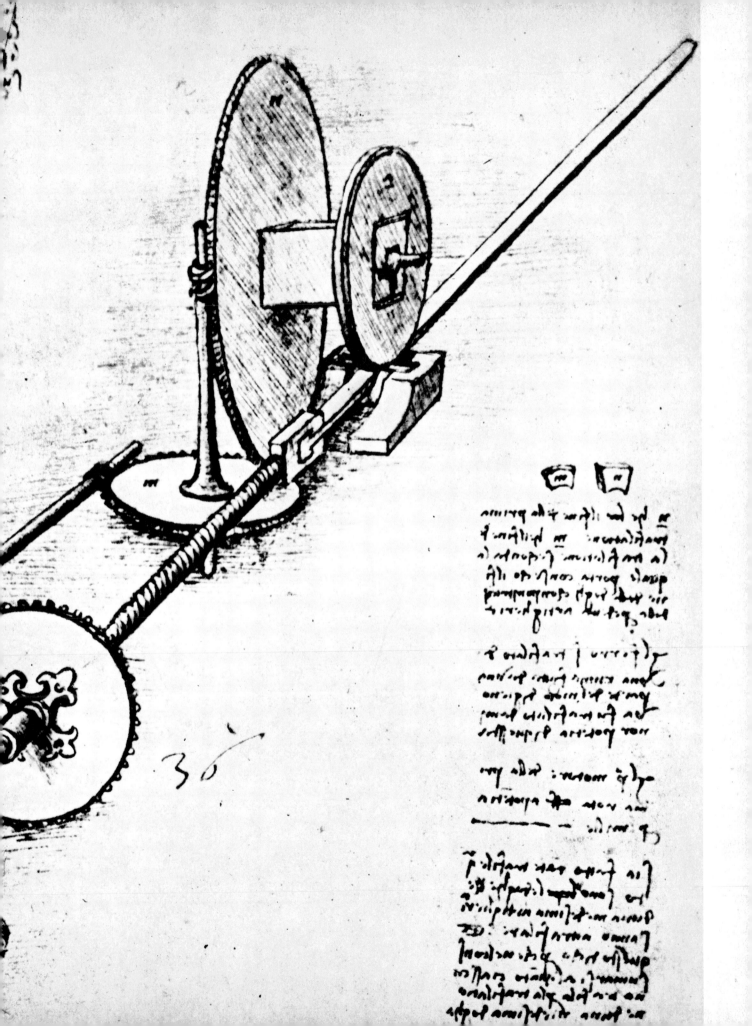

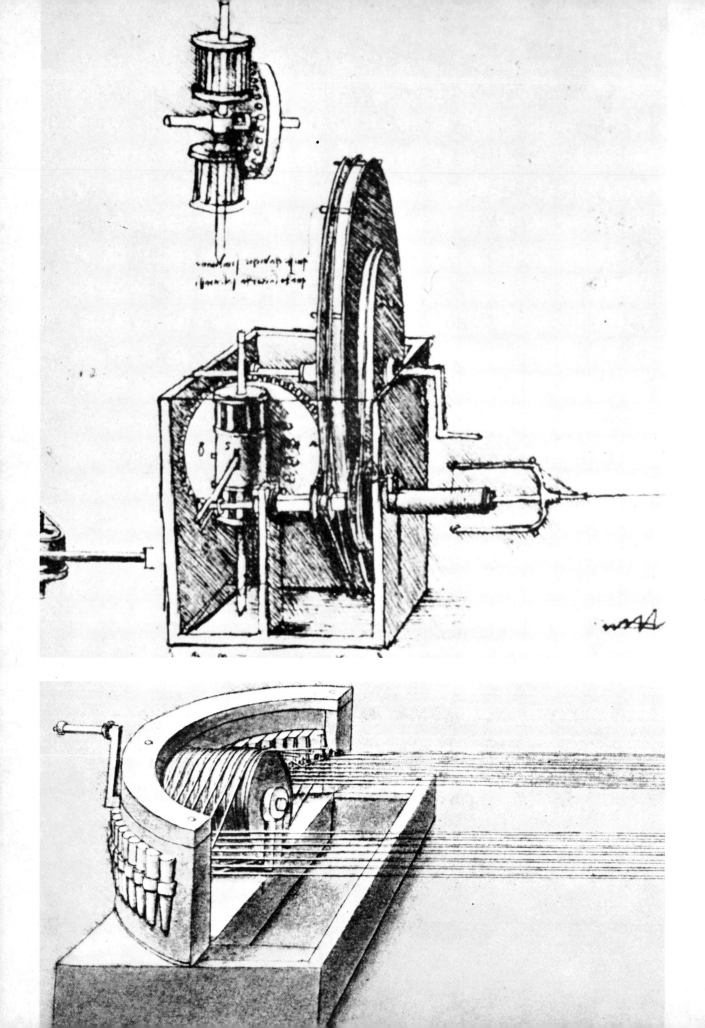

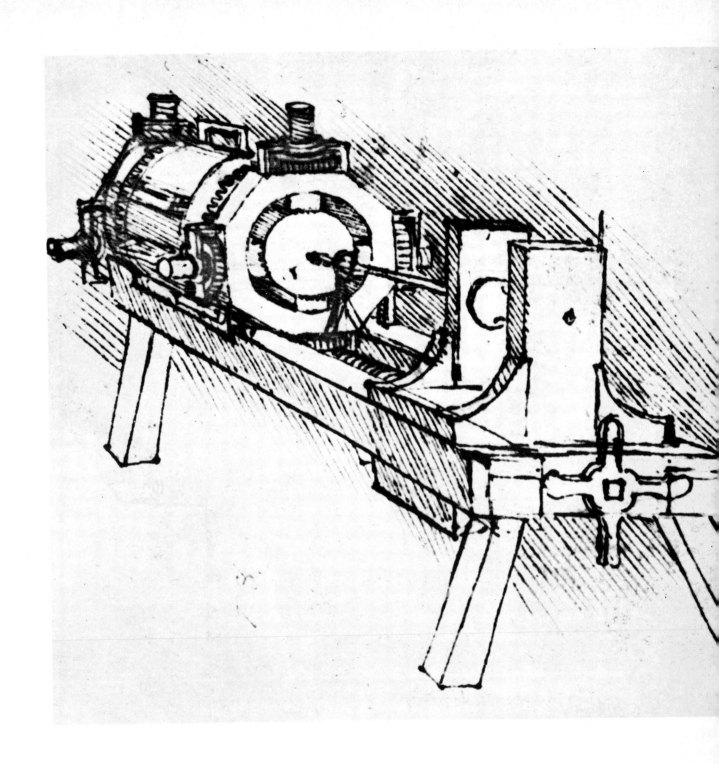

*Top left: studies for a thread-winding
machine.
Bottom: this rope-winding device
involves the use of several spindles.
Below: design for a drill.*

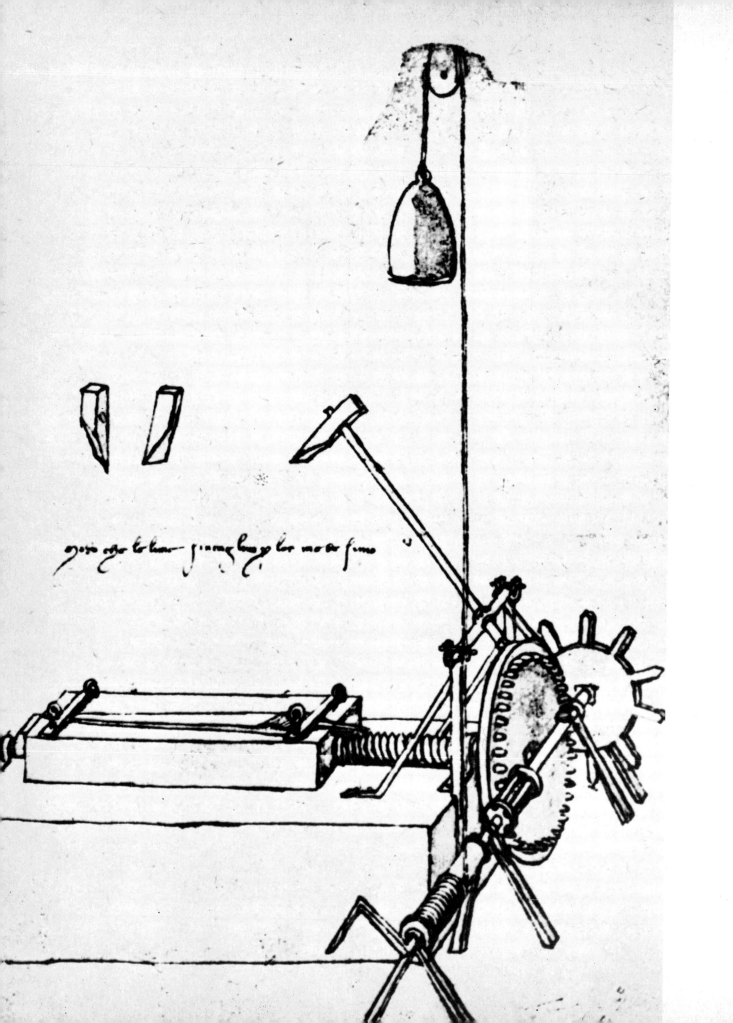

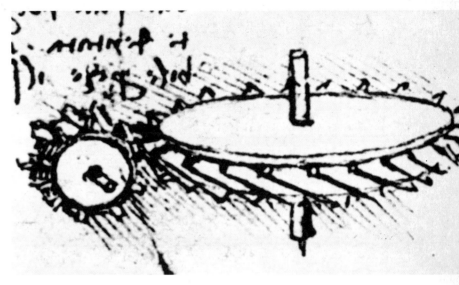

Left: device for cutting of files, with stopping mechanism.
Facing: studies of assorted gear wheels.
Above: note a special feature of these gears: they are helicoidal.
Below: study of differential mechanisms.

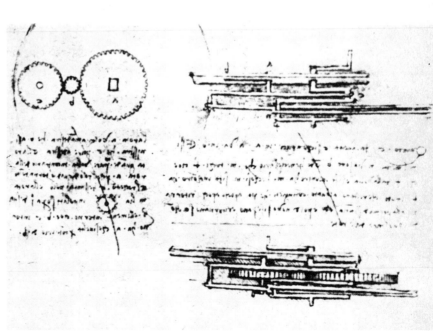

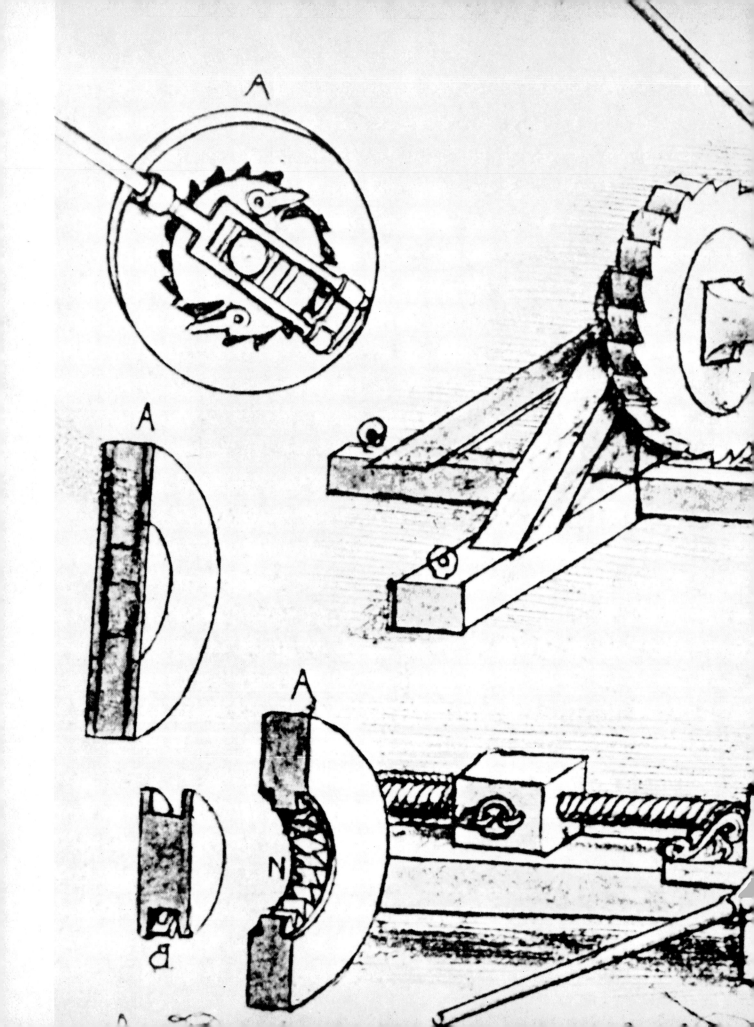

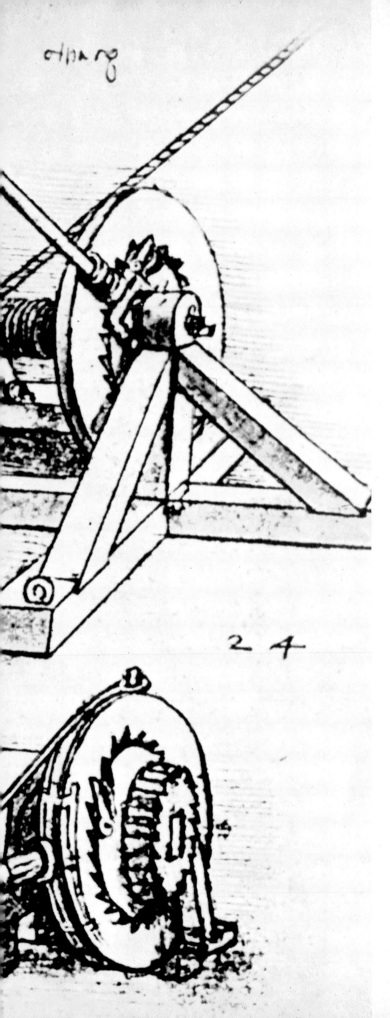

A winch, with detail of jack-lift operation.

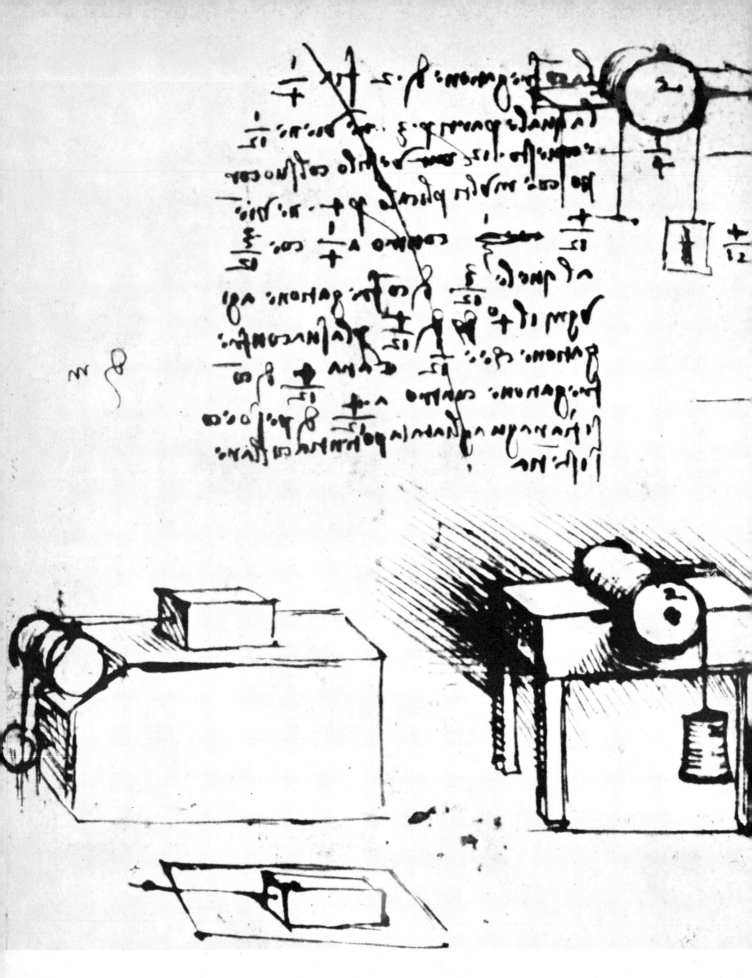

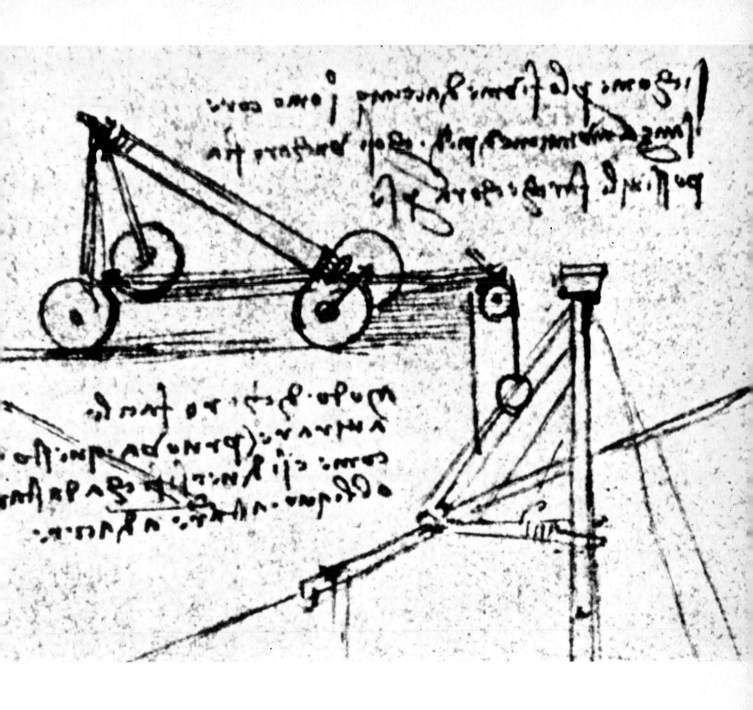

Left: a study of friction on flat or mobile surfaces.
Above: self-propelled vehicle.
Following pages: here Leonardo gives us a graphic account of the laws of traction, based on the work of an ox in the fields.

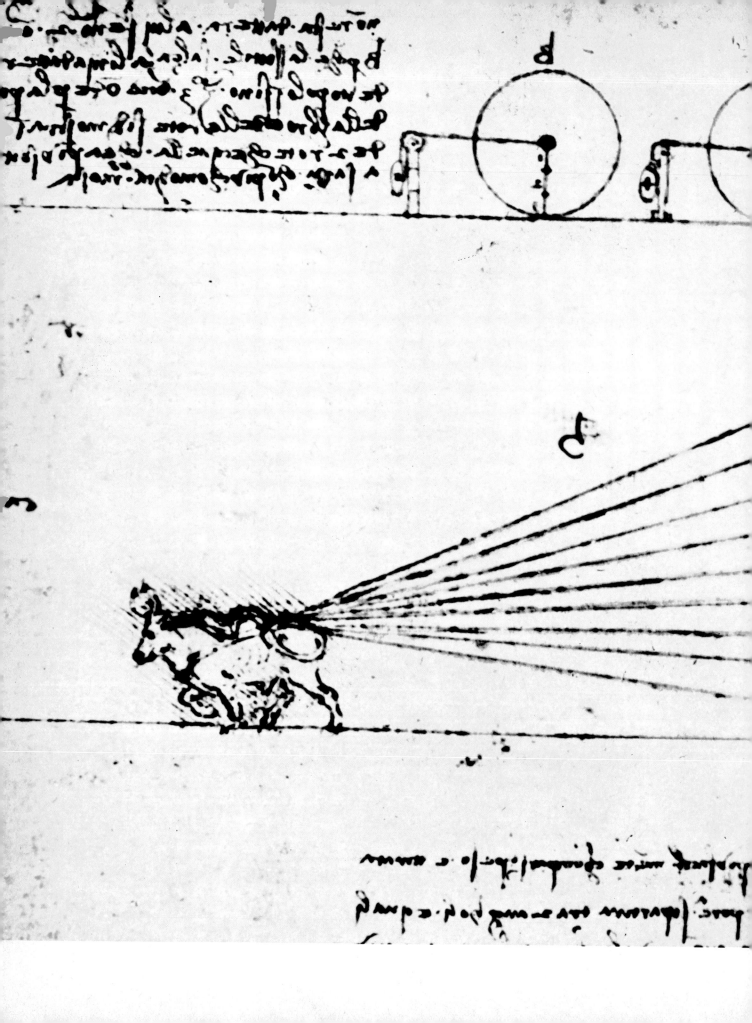

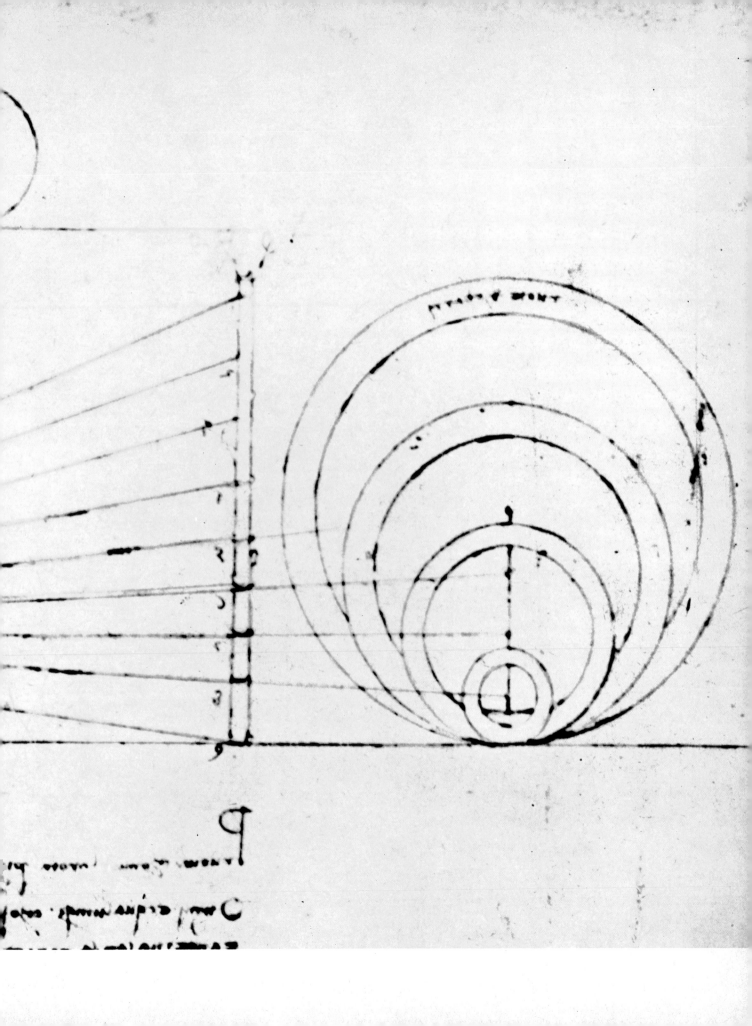

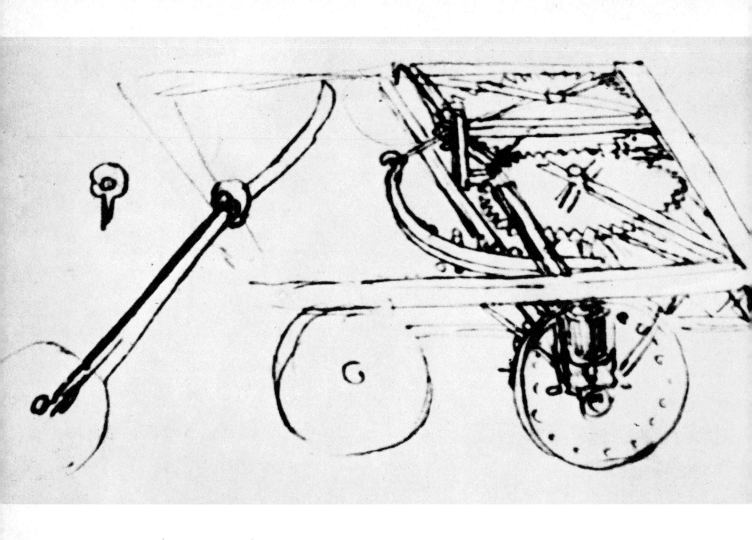

On these two pages: design for a self-propelled vehicle with differential transmission. Two views: perspective and two-dimensional.

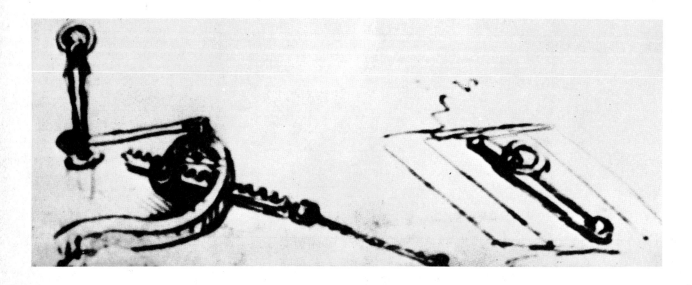

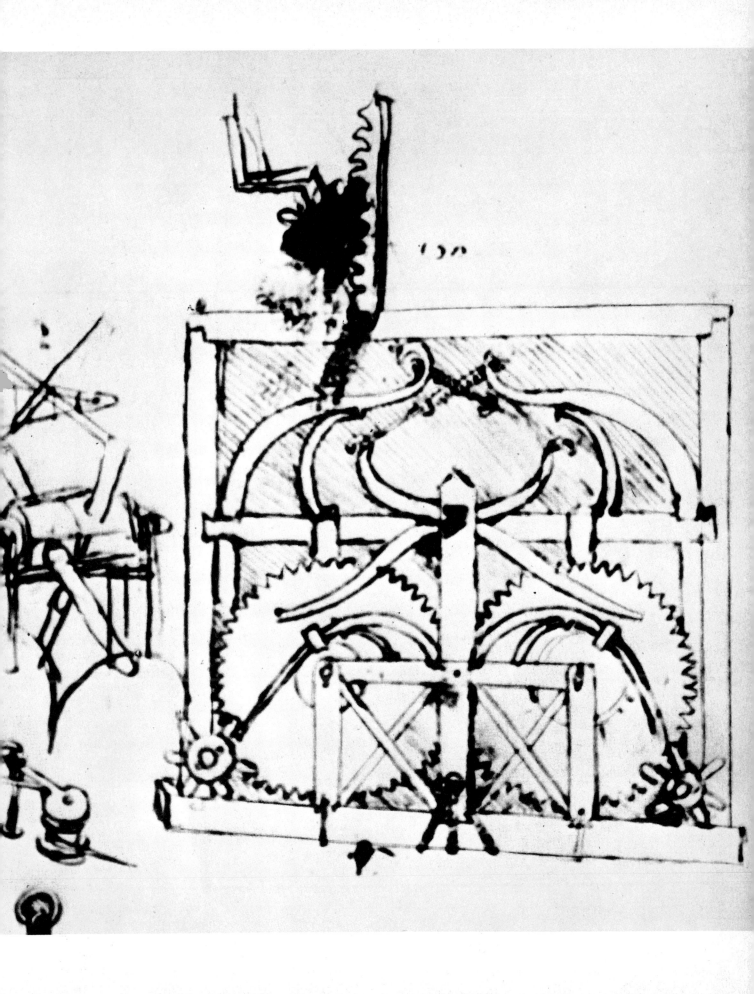

*Above: Leonardo also devised a...
bicycle.
Right: two machines for measuring the number of paces taken by
a person walking.*

volta intorno b 10. co la rota del ...ro
onde viene nossa di ...ro b. 3 e ½
ella prodasse ... hosso di ... sia
multiplicato p. 3 e ½ ...
... genal. summa ... 10
... a ... vn ... modo
... el ... aqua ... et
... pilia ... colsuo ...
... ro ... ilquale a 22 ...
... ro ... ro molti pli
... p. 3 e ½ ... 22
... la regola del. 3. ... 22
... 88

Assorted weapons.

The craft-based prosperity of the Italian cities of the Renaissance had led Leonardo to seek ways of achieving industrial yield from machines through automation.

His studies of military problems derived from the warfare between rival cities which behaved like mini-states.

It should not be forgotten that the princes who used Leonardo's services enlisted him in their courts with the title of Military Expert and Engineer. They thus clearly intended that he should devote his inventive genius essentially to bolstering their military power.

In fact he once again followed his natural instinct, neglecting strategy and tactics and taking an interest only in the problems of military architecture, and, above all, in the creation of new weapons based primarily on an understanding of the laws of ballistics.

In 1346, at Crécy, the English had used, for the first time in Europe, cannons firing stone balls propelled by the force of exploding gunpowder.

This development was, however, purely empirical: ballistics remained unknown to contemporary scientists and military men alike.

This was the direction in which Leonardo applied his efforts, before producing improved projectiles and firearms by means of the 'laws' he had discovered.

In actual fact he merely anticipated those laws, as he relied solely on his infallible eye and his instinctive intuition in dealing with the major principles of ballistics. His knowledge of mathematics was inadequate as a means of expressing these things in scientific terms. It was rather as an inspired humanist that he perceived them intuitively, while being unable to formulate them as a scientist.

Even so, he was the first to enunciate the parabolic trajectory of projectiles. He was the first to measure the penetrating power of projectiles by demonstrating that the penetration into the ground of an arrow shot vertically into the air varies directly with the altitude it reaches, and, therefore, with the release of the bow. In an experiment he even sent a rocket-powered cannonball to a height of nearly ten thousand feet: an astonishing accomplishment in his day and one which, in the absence of aerial targets, is evidence of his purely scientific quest for knowledge.

He also fully realized the essential role of air resistance; but it was not until 1687 that Newton gave it a precise formulation.

Notwithstanding such distinct empiricism, Leonardo worked to transform the firepower of Renaissance armies.

In all his research, expressed in an avalanche of drawings, one continually sees his concern for precision, efficiency and speed.

His aim was to make everything simpler and more reliable.

To begin with, he designed and improved the traditional weapons which had emerged from the Middle Ages: halberd, mace, lance, cross-bow.

Quite early on, however, he sought to change them and apply to them his ballistic discoveries and his obsession with speed.

His first conversions look like an updated version of Roman and medieval devices:

Catapults arranged in arrays and discharged by sledge-hammer blows delivered simultaneously by a row of men.

Giant slingshots tautened by extra-strong or multiple springs released by the centrifugal force of a swivel.

Rapid-firing crossbows, the impressive weapon of a visionary. An enormous treadmill was to be powered by a team of well-built men pedalling endlessly on steps built, for greater efficiency, on the outer rim of the wheel. A conventional crossbow was attached to each diagonal. A man stationed in the middle discharged each crossbow as it came level with him. A braking system made it possible to slow down the rotation, and a slot provided a view of the target.

Giant ballista, a huge crossbow mounted on six wheels, canted to absorb the shock of recoil. The 'shoe' containing the missile was held in position by two wedges; the bow was drawn by a system of worms and gears and released by striking a pin.

Siege equipement. While devising the ideal fortifications for impregnable citadels, Leonardo was also busy inventing ways of taking those same fortresses.

He made a series of drawings showing folding hooked ladders for scaling ramparts; articulated bridges for crossing moats; platforms on pillars and wheels capable of looking over battlements and enabling attackers to fire inside the citadels.

These ideas were not, in themselves, original, being merely an up-to-date version of ancient Roman machines, and distant forerunners of the work of our modern military engineers.

The new phenomenon of artillery was of the greatest interest to Leonardo.

There was a great deal to be done to improve this new queen of the battlefield.

First of all, he devised breech-loading rather than muzzle-loading cannons.

Then he sought to cool them more quickly by immersion in vats of flowing water. In this way, in a battery of several guns, one would be cooling while a second was being loaded and a third fired.

This problem of the rate of fire was a major concern of Leonardo's.

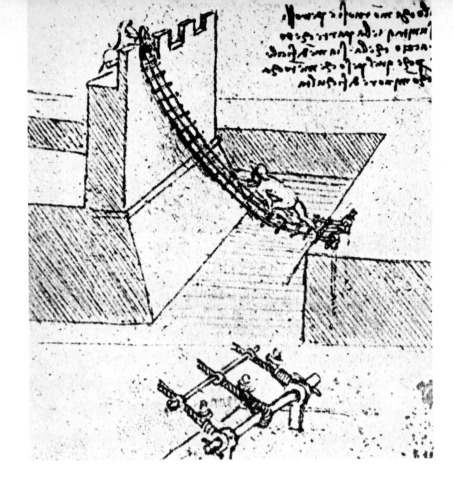

How to attack a fortified wall...

To cope with it he invented a whole series of weapons which may be described as 'automatic' – clusters of a dozen cannons, mounted on the same carriage, and capable of being fired successively or at the same time. These weapons were, in fact, an early form of our earliest machine-guns.

In this same sphere he designed giant howitzers identical to those used during the War of Secession and spitting out a hail of shot.

The best of these scatter-type weapons was a kind of shot-firing 'organ' mounted on a drum; this was not an accurate weapon.

Lastly, he even worked on the casting of cannons, which had previously been molded in a number of segments banded together in the same way as the sections of a barrel. He proposed either to cast them in a single piece, as he had in the case of Sforza's giant horse, or to make them from a single sheet of metal stretched out and rolled in a spiral.

Perhaps his most advanced new ideas was the replacement of exploding gunpowder by steam power: the breech would be placed in a hot brazier which would make it red hot; water would be inserted into the breech, promptly turn to steam and the resulting enormous pressure would propel the cannonball.

Having thus modified weapons, it was clearly necessary to do something about projectiles.

Leonardo's exuberant activity in this field was both eccentric and prophetic: incendiary cannonballs, a new form of the ancients''Greek fire'' ; trick shells, the ancestors of the gas weapons of 1914; shells

83

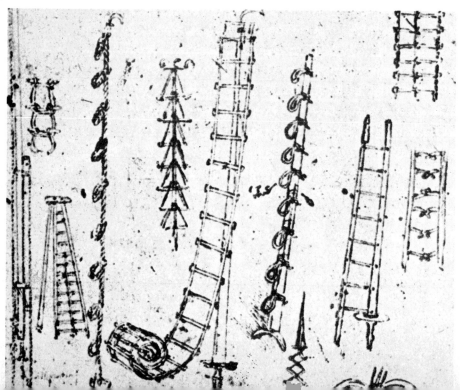

*Above: a combat tank.
Left: a type of ladder for scaling fortress walls.
Right-hand page, bottom: plans for the defense of a fortress.*

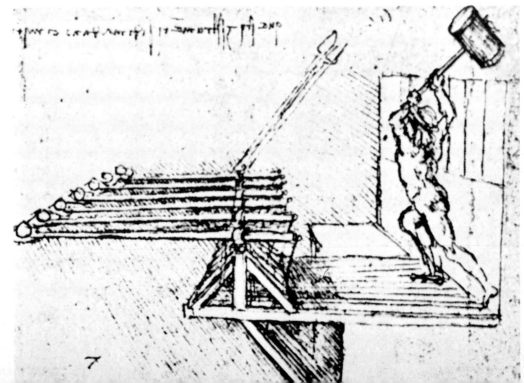

7

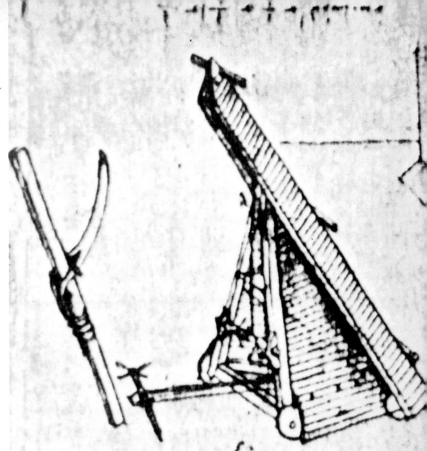

Left: the response to the technology shown on page 83: a device with which to topple the ladders of assailants. Right: platformed vehicle enabling troops to storm a fortified wall.

equipped with hollow antennae filled with gunpowder and exploding on impact; hollow cannonballs filled with gunpowder and rendered fragile so as to burst on impact scattering their pulverized contents, like modern shrapnel weapons.

However, in order to derive the maximum benefit from these new weapons and these sophisticated projectiles, a practical, fast and reliable firing system was needed. This was perhaps his most valuable contribution.

First of all he greatly improved the old method for firing the arquebus, accelerating the previously two-stage process by having ignition and detonation occur simultaneously.

But he went further than this and devised a revolutionary wheellock: pressure on the trigger set in motion a pyrite-bearing arm which ignited the gunpowder.

This method, which was much more reliable, but also but more expensive than flint, was not adopted in armaments until centuries later.

He was also centuries ahead of his times with his conception of an armored vehicle to replace the excessively vulnerable horse. This sort of giant metallic turtle on four wheels would clearly enjoy enviable advantages on the battlefield.

There can be no doubt that Leonardo displayed exceptional powers of imagination in the military sphere; like so many modern scientists he placed his creative genius in the service of war, which he actually denounced as a 'bestial folly'.

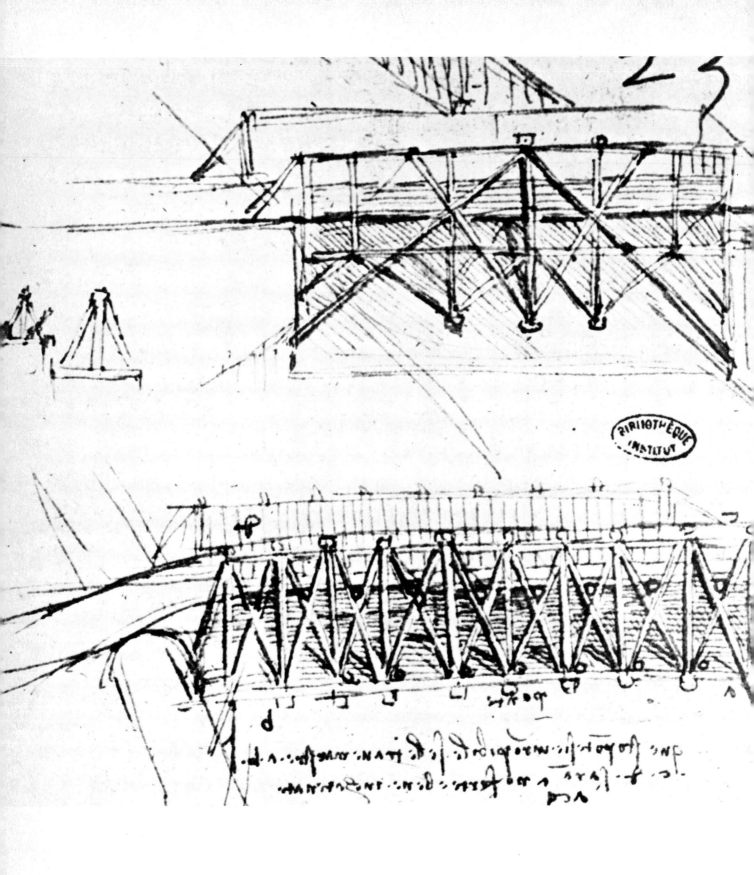

Above: model of a
temporary bridge.

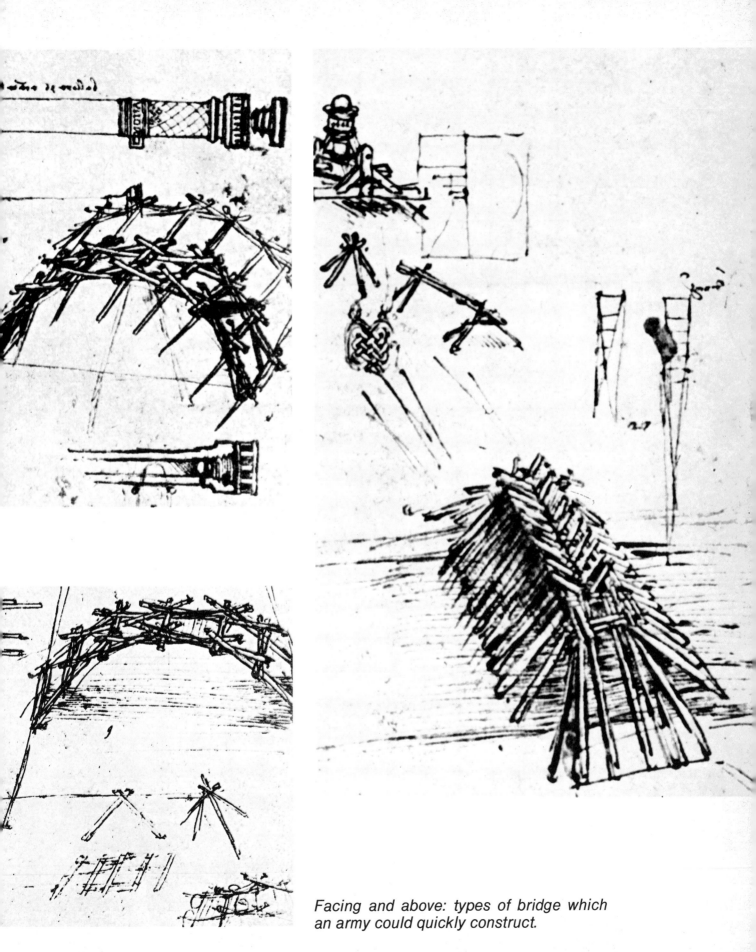

*Facing and above: types of bridge which
an army could quickly construct.*

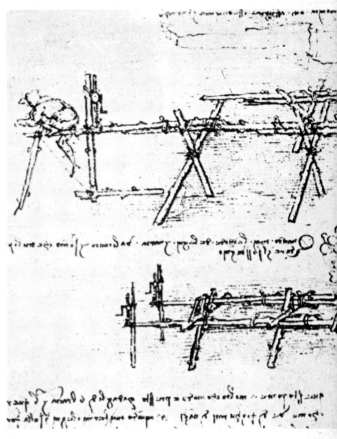

Left: two models of bridges based on the parabolic principle.
Above: another provisional bridge for the army.

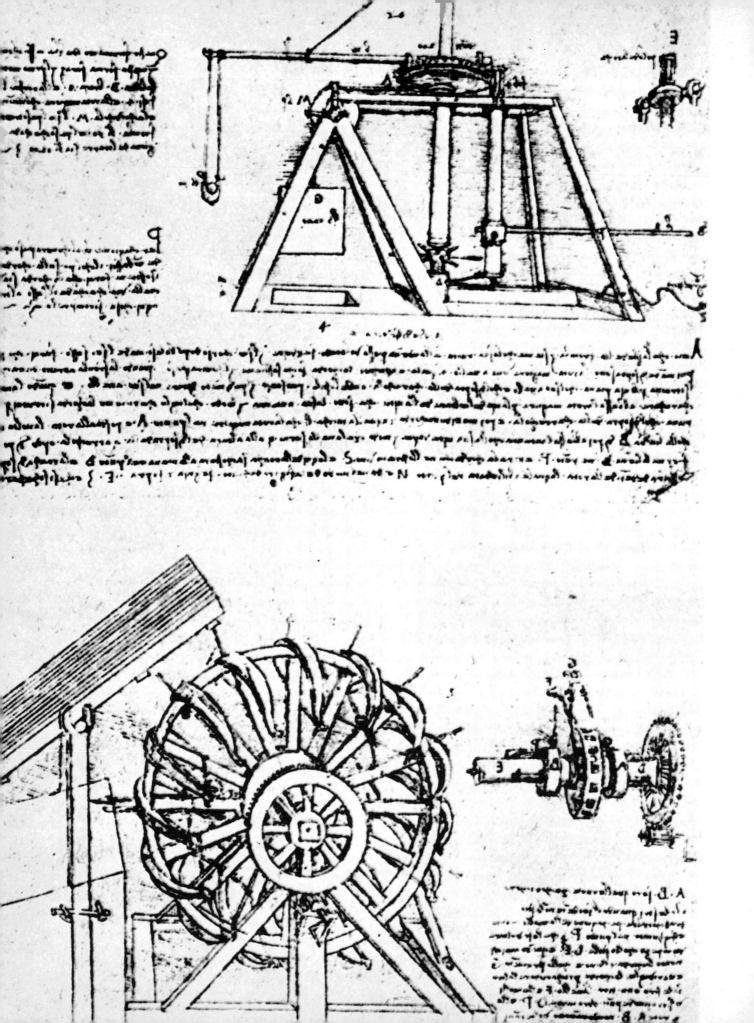

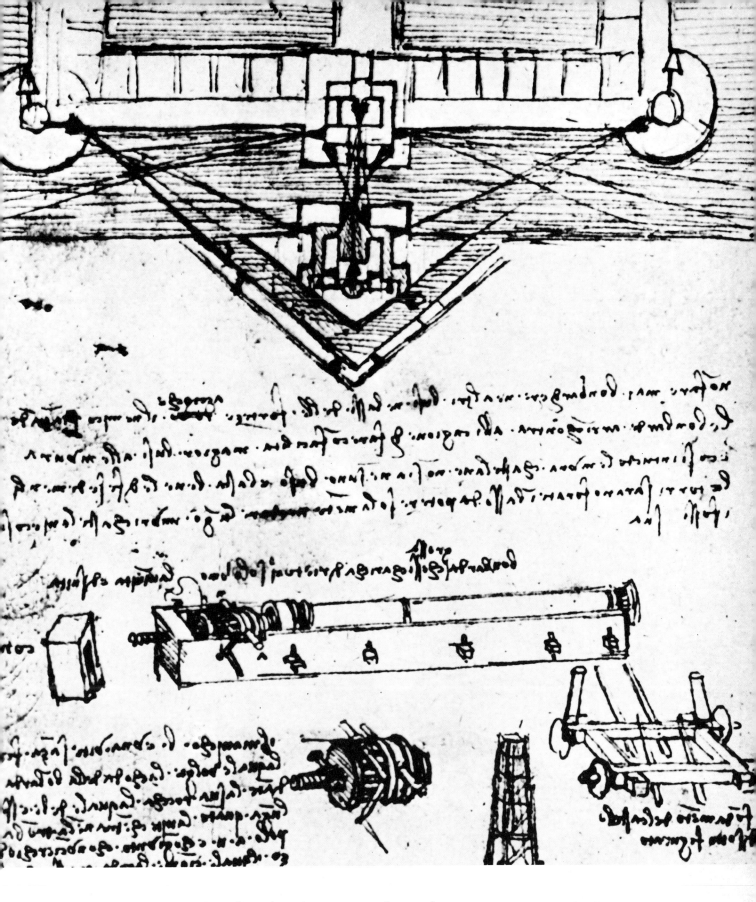

Left: improved catapult and spring-powered crossbow.
Above: device intended for use in artillery emplaced at a corner of
the Sforza castle, Milan.

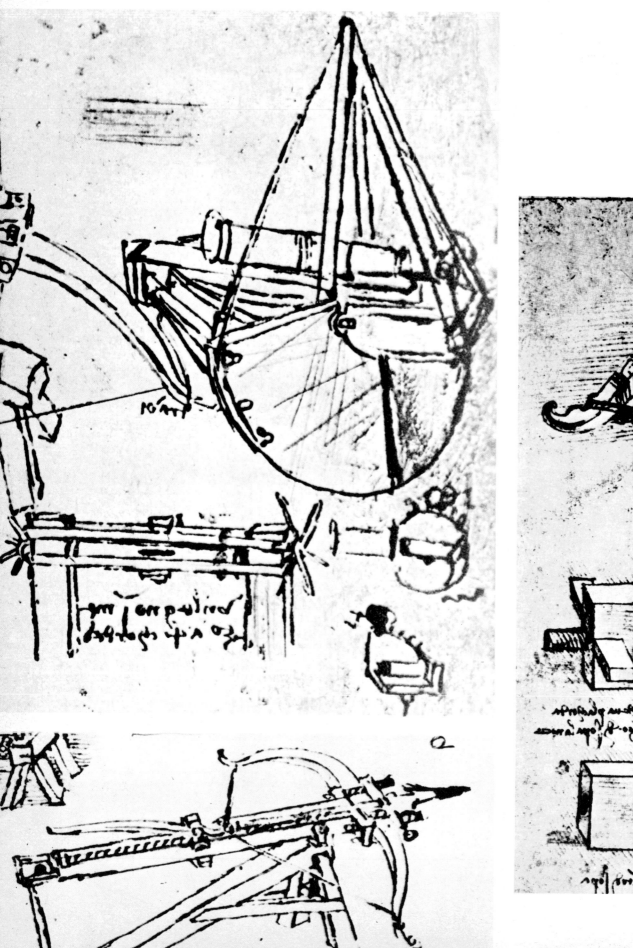

On these two pages, various types of crossbow: note that the giant model shown below is mounted on wheels.

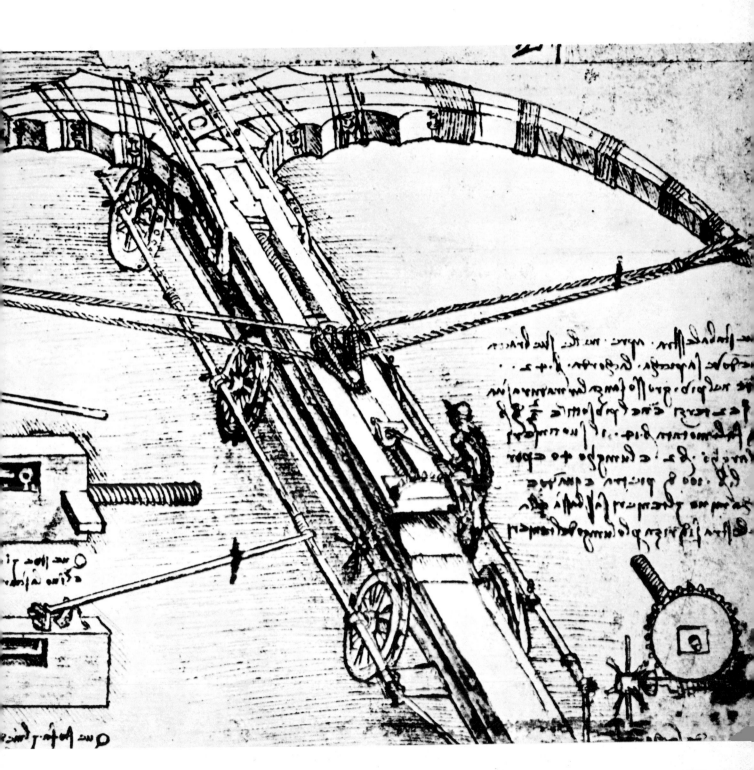

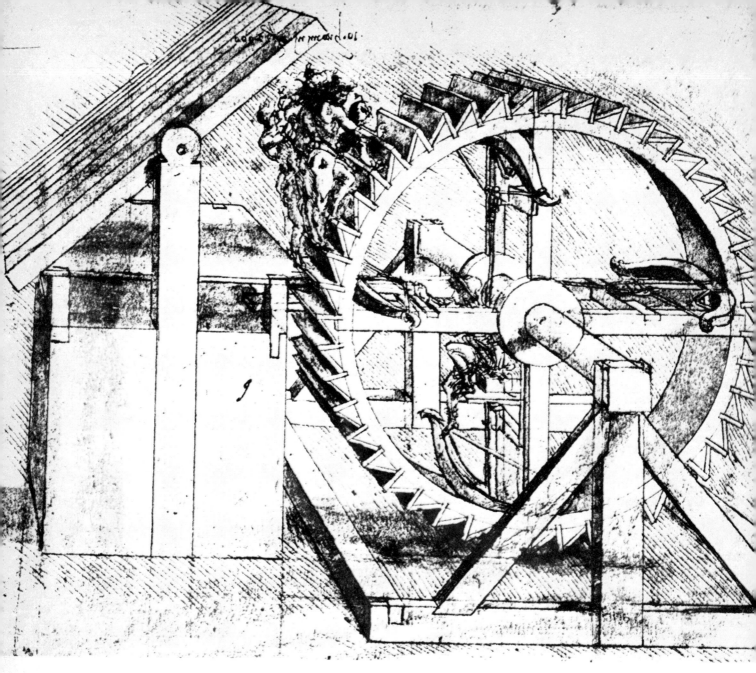

Above: crossbows secured to a wheel to ensure a rapid rate of fire.
Left: Leonardo's idea of an explosive bomb.
Right: cross-section of a bombard with the design of the balls and their motion.

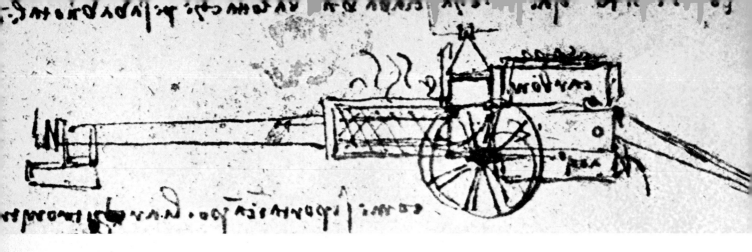

Above: design for a steam cannon.
Below: design for the manufacture of a cannon barrel.
Right-hand page: a famous plate: scene inside a cannon foundry.

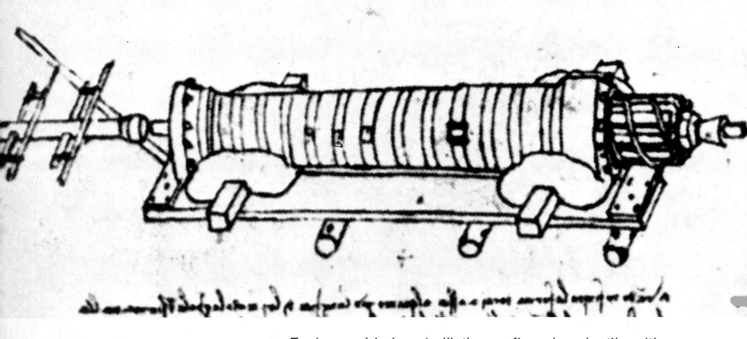

Facing and below: ballistics: a finned projectile with a warhead, and another type of finned projectile.

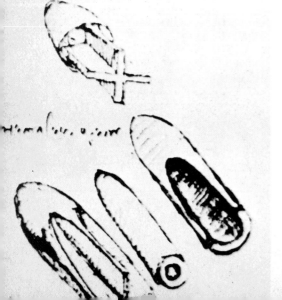

Facing and right: a cannon and a bombard in firing position.
Below and bottom right: projectiles in action.
Bottom of this page: two cannons mounted on a gun carriage.

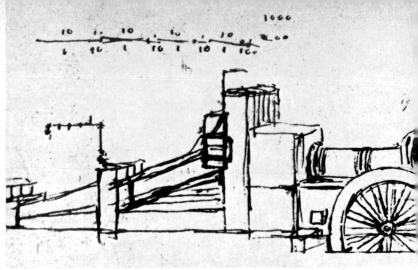

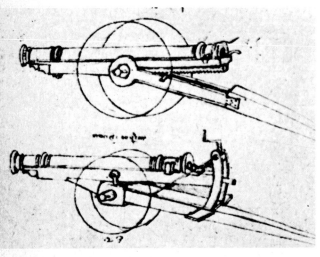

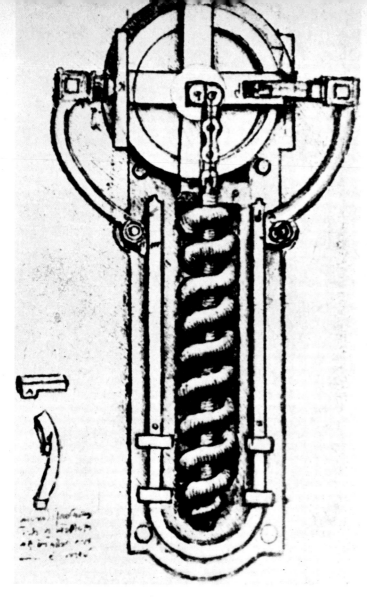

Facing, left: installation for hoisting military hardware.
Bottom of page: various designs for cannon.
Right: military hardware including what is thought to be the design for a sort of machine gun.

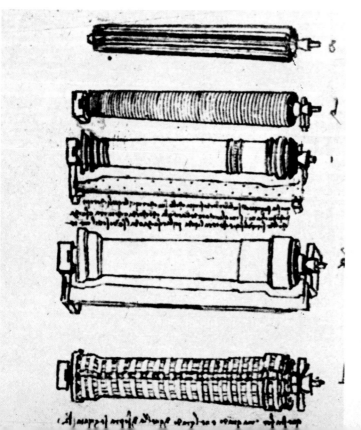

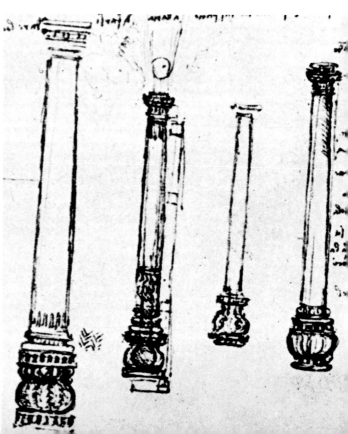

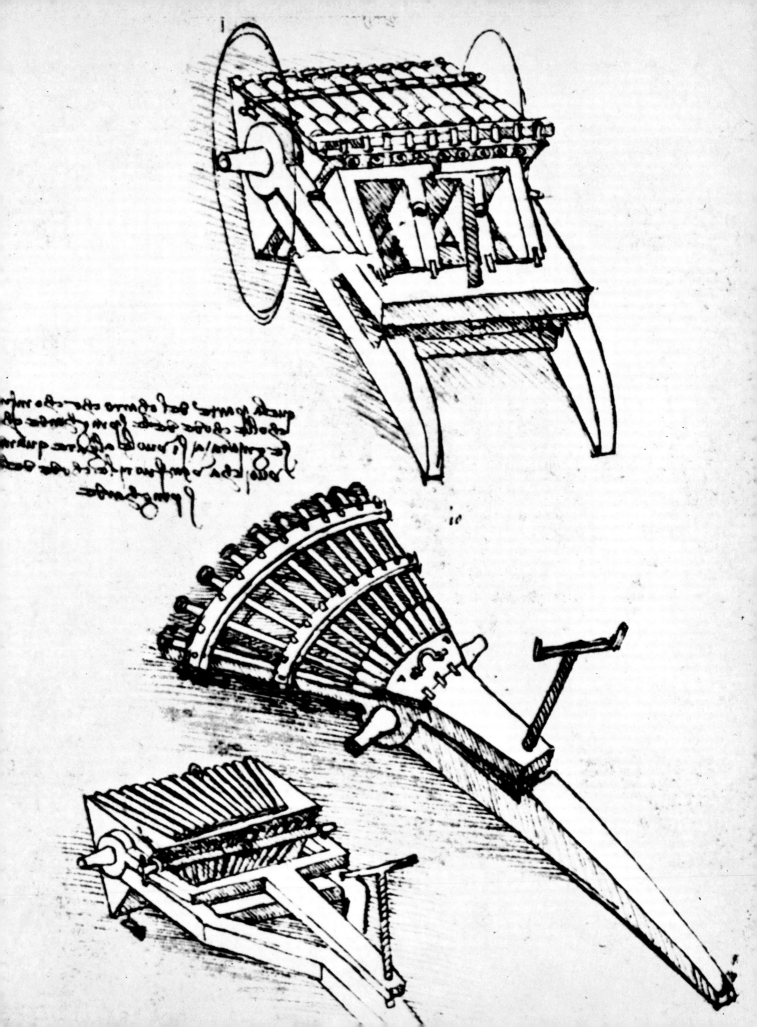

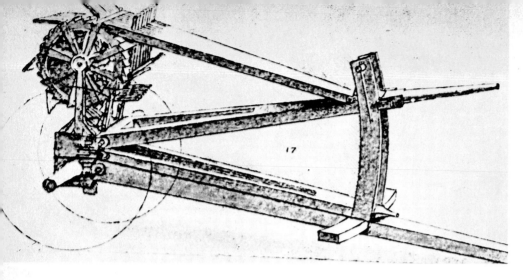

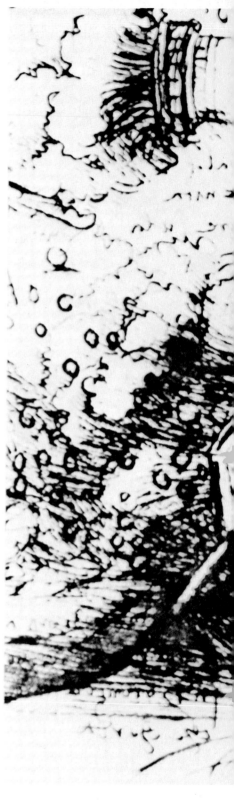

As his research proceeded, Leonardo added to his studies of various types of crossbow this automatic reloading device.

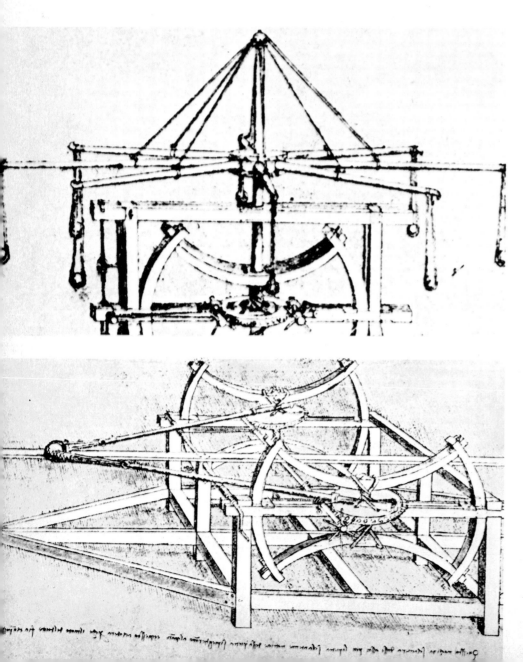

Bottom left: mortar designed to use either explosive projectiles or ordinary stones as ammunition. The figure shown above is not easily identified.
Above: on this page of sketches can be seen a naval vessel, and also, at the top of the figure, a model of a new cannon.

Credits : Giraudon, Paris –
Roger-Viollet, Paris –
Editoriale Gemini, Milano –
British Museum, Londres –
Royal Library, Windsor Castle –
Bibliothèque Nationale, Paris.

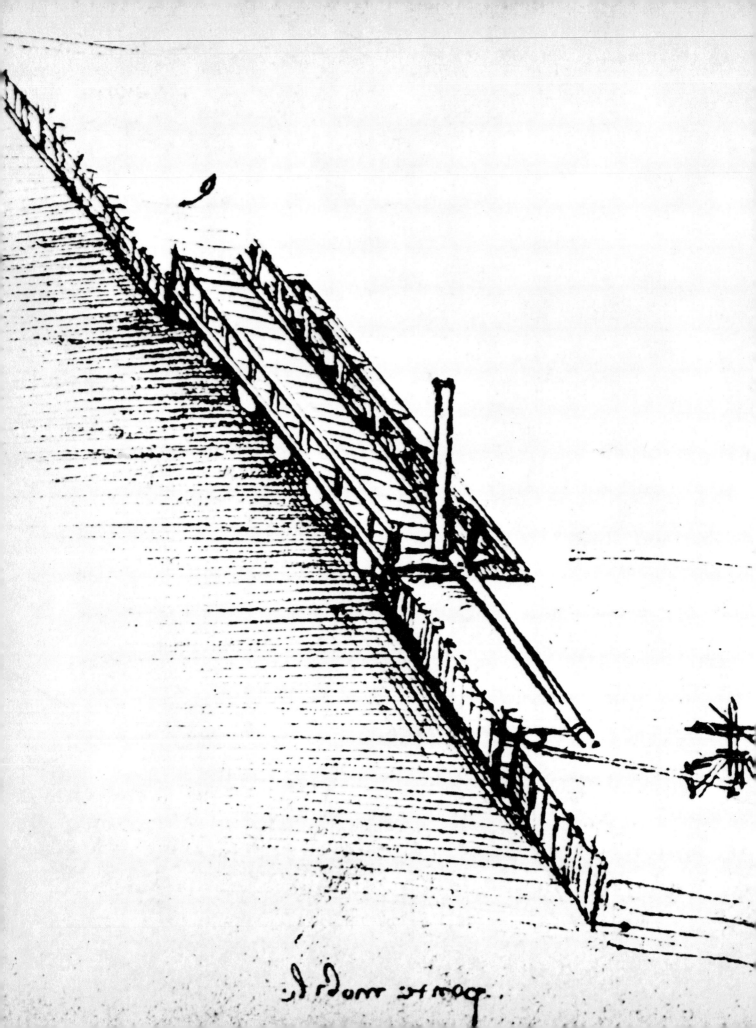